# RELATIONSHIPS
### AND
# MARRIAGES
## Gods Way

# RELATIONSHIPS AND MARRIAGES

## *Gods Way*

DENBURK GREGORY & VERONICA GREGORY

Copyright © 2022 by Denburk Gregory & Veronica Gregory.

Library of Congress Control Number:    2021924645

HARDBACK:            978-1-957575-03-2
PAPERBACK:           978-1-957575-02-5
EBOOK:               978-1-957575-04-9

All rights reserved. No part of this publication may be reproduced, distributed, or transmitted in any form or by any electronic or mechanical means, without the prior written permission of the publisher, except in the case of brief quotations embodied in critical reviews and certain other noncommercial uses permitted by copyright law.

**Ordering Information:**

For orders and inquiries, please contact:
1-888-404-1388
www.goldtouchpress.com
book.orders@goldtouchpress.com

Printed in the United States of America

# PREFACE

We have come to the knowledge that many believers "Christians" are divorcing their spouses, and this needs to stop in the precious name of Jesus. We heard the preachers minister the word of God to us weekly and the delivering of the message as God has given it. Haven't they been teaching how important it is for Christians to maintain a good relationship with their spouse and children and maintain their marriages?

Because of relationship break-ups and abuse in the marriage, we need to remind them what the word of God has said to us and is still speaking to all of us until we die. That a husband must love his wife as Jesus Christ loves humanity and died for them and that the wife should submit herself to her own husband according to the word of God. This command is for all husbands and wives, and our problem has been disobedience to God and His Son Jesus Christ.

We have learned that the divorce rate in the United States is declining, which is very good, but one divorce is too much because of the pain and financial instability it causes in some divorces. Many children go through psychological distress, knowing that they are no longer living with their two parents. According to a study, about forty (40) percent of marriages end in divorce in 2019; this is very high; we need to do better. Over a hundred thousand people got a divorce in 2017, and this is very bad when we think about what the Lord God has said about divorce. Divorce is not an American problem; instead, it is a worldwide epidemic of families torn apart because the spouses did not invest quality time and work hard to keep their marriage intact, many tried, however, they did it without involving Jesus Christ in their situation.

This book will help improve many relationships and marriages if each spouse begins to follow the recipe or guideline-based upon God's word for their lives. This book is for married couples; and for all the single people in a relationship waiting to be married one day. We use God's word as the foundation upon which this writing is based and a common-sense approach to life experiences. What are the methods? These are only a few of them:

**Love:** Love is the foundation of every relationship and marriage. Many may say it is money, sex, and material things, but those things will perish here or then, but love is everlasting and will never die because it is spiritual. As you read this book, you will know that the love we are talking about is not just words, but it comes with many different attributes to show that you genuinely love your spouse. We must have God's love in us because we cannot give what we do not have, and since we do not have it, we cannot give it to those who are supposed to receive it.

**Understanding:** Understanding is vitally important to all because of the value of information that you will learn. Knowledge and experience without wisdom, people can take you for a fool. Having a sense of what to do and what not to do makes your day and life more manageable. You will know what to do and what not to do because now you understand Wisdom and Knowledge. Without understanding is like a foolish person walking in the desert without water.

**Compromise:** In a relationship, the spouses and those not married need to learn how to make a sensible compromise to live their lives without problem and confusion. There is nothing wrong with agreeing with someone's point of view or decision that does not align with yours if it does not cause hurt, death, or destruction, which is sin. Compromise should never be one-sided only to benefit an individual, but it should always point to helping those involved directly or indirectly.

**Being Honest:** Honesty is a vital ingredient of any relationship, personal, or business. There is no need to hide things from your spouse when we speak of honesty, such as a secret bank account or buying items in secret without wanting your spouse to know about it. Yes, there is nothing wrong with buying a surprise gift for your spouse or friend that will surprise the wedding anniversary, birthday, Mother's Day, Father's Day, and so forth, not those mentions; instead, spending money on someone and hiding the receipt from your spouse. However, there is so much more in a relationship or marriage, you must remember and know that you are no longer a single person, and you will need to make some necessary adjustments in your life so that there will be no mistrust.

# CHAPTER ONE

## *The Purpose of the writers*

Greetings to all from God our Father and the Lord Jesus Christ to whom all glory, honor, and praise belongeth unto because They are from everlasting to everlasting, and from everlasting to everlasting, the Lord is God, Amen. Be it known to all of us that the Lord God Almighty is the God of all knowledge, wisdom, and understanding of hearts, and He is a God that decerns our thoughts.

In the late twentieth century into the twenty-first century, people have become so highly sensitive about so many things that sometimes it becomes a problem to speak to them. If you say this, they think you are harsh; if you say that, they believe the same. Are we, as adults, become babies? In this book, please know there will be words used that may be considered a passive voice. Do not be offended because dealing with sin should not be treated as an egg. Please, the worse words you will ever hear in your entire life will be, if you died in your sins, and Jesus will say to you, depart from me ye workers of iniquity.

This book is not only for the Christian community; instead, it is for all humanity upon the face of the earth. There are two types of people or groups in the world, the Spiritual and the non-spiritual.

The spiritual people have a connection with their God and not those who have a form of spirituality, believe in God and His Son, Jesus Christ, and have surrendered their lives unto Jesus Christ, the Savior of the world. However, a mixed multitude of people say that they are saved, "meaning being born again," but they are not living the authentic life for Jesus Christ. Yes, you believe in Jesus; believing is not enough; you must align your life according to the word of God, and we encourage you to do so before it is too late for you.

The next are those who are not saved, meaning they have not surrendered their life unto Jesus Christ; they are not blood washed by Jesus Christ of Nazareth. This group of people had not yet experienced regeneration, meaning "the new birth," which is being born again by the Spirit of God. As stated before, many people believe in God, but that is not enough. **St. John 3: 1-12.** also, they are living a life of sin.

Why this book? Because it is based upon the word of God, and the word of God is sound doctrine. It is also time for all of us to truly take time out and reflect on God's holy word and see if we are applying His words to our lives daily because God's word is always correct. Not because we do not understand the truth of God's holy word; it does not mean that the word of God is not relevant in our lives today.

We wrote this book because we believe that it is full time the world comes to the absolute truth in acknowledging the Almighty God and His dear begotten Son Jesus Christ and what **They** have to say about relationships and marriages. All of us, who are upon the face of the earth, many of us are living a life of lies and never come to the truth, and we need to line up and do that which the Lord God has commanded us to do so that we can reign with Christ Jesus for eternity. As we line up and make the necessary adjustments in our lives to please God, we will experience His **Presence** and **Favor** in our lives.

Throughout our lifetime in this present world or until the Lord God come and do away with the evil that is in this world, we will continue in some ways to experience wickedness because of sin and the evil that is in the heart of humanity. Many human beings do not know God's will; therefore, because of the lack of knowledge, many of us live our lives not knowing that we are living our lives in significant error. It is always God's plan that all human beings will seek Him and get His **Wisdom**, **Knowledge,** and **understanding** of who He truly is.

We believe that this book will help many of you, if not all, to come to the truth of what the Lord God wants us to know about relationships and marriage. Many of us have asked others what the secret is in their marriage, that is wonderful to get insight, and there is nothing wrong with asking because we all learn from one another. Nevertheless, how many of us went to enquire from the Creator of all things and the One who establishes marriage in the first place and knows the hearts of humanity to find out the real secret of marriage? The Lord God has the answers to all your questions, and you can find them in the Bible, and the Holy Spirit will guide us to the formula for having a successful relationship. As you read the word and study the word of God and search it out to know, the Lord will reveal Himself to you, and the blessing of the Lord will find you as you obey Him.

In this case, the Lord God is the only one who can genuinely instruct us, mainly because of humanity's hearts, how to live and experience an enjoyable and prosperous married life if we follow His prescriptions. If we need to know the nature of God, read His word. If we need to know the mind of God, read His word, and if we need to know the will of God for humanity, read the Bible. The Bible is our guide in revealing to us everlasting punishment or everlasting life; all of us need to have one for ourselves. It contains instruction from the Lord God for life and death, for success and disappointments. When humanity follows God's commandments and keeps His covenant, we will live and not die, but we will die if we refuse to obey the Lord God according to His word in the Bible.

Study the word of God, and you will know how to please Him. Try the recipe from the Lord that He has given to all humanity so that we will know His will. Give God's recipe a try and apply the ingredients to your life. In the Bible, there are written instructions for life and not death. Used them by applying the instructions carefully and see if you or we will not have a successful life like many others experiencing remarkable, excellent, successful, and stressless relationships and marriages even at this present time. Will trouble and trial come to test you? Sure, as long as we are alive on this earth, something or someone will always want to bring negative vibes into our lives. When they show up in your life, rebuke them in the name of the Lord Jesus Christ of Nazareth.

We, the human race by nature, inherit a rebellious spirit from our forefather, Adam. Because of it, we always want to sin, which is to have things our way instead of pleasing the Lord. We think it is okay to do what we please and whenever we please without realizing that our actions may be hurting others. Some of us will not want to give God's recipe for Relationships and Marriages a try because we don't want to accept the truth from the Lord our God about the proper way we ought to live by conducting ourselves as civilized people. Why? Because for too long, we have gotten caught up in our **Traditions** and **Customs,** and some of them are destroying people's lives and bringing fort unhappiness to the home. We know that many may not want to accept what this writing is all about, but that's okay; sometimes it takes time to adjust to new things, but that's essential as long as we get there without being offended. Therefore, let us not be afraid of what you are about to experience in this book; it is not to hurt you or make things worse; instead, it is to help get you to do the will of Almighty God, who is our heavenly Father and His Son the Lord Jesus Christ. Please remember this very carefully; every human being is God's child. Yet, not all of us will reign with Christ Jesus for eternity because many refuse to accept Jesus Christ as their Lord and Savior.

Many of us do not like change, but some changes are good for us; that is why this book's writing will help many relationships and marriages flourish and be less stressful, but you must align yourself in obedience to the word of the Lord for your life. Sometimes the truth hurts a lot about what is said; nevertheless, we must tell the truth in love and wisdom with humility at all times. Therefore, in love, we share this writing with you about relationships and marriages, so we took this bold step to write about it. We pray that the Lord Jesus will bless each person as He favors your going out and coming in. Remember, every good thing comes from above. As each of us makes the necessary adjustments in our life according to God's plan and purposes for us, then you will come to experience a beautiful and blessed married life in the Lord God in Jesus' name. This writing is not about the writers; instead, it is all about **God's Plan and Purposes** for all human beings from the four corners of the world so that all of us will agree with His **Perfect Plan** as He has planned it before the foundation of the world.

For too long now, humanity has been living in ignorance of God's will, and many do not know God's will for themself; many have perished, and they have no future with Jesus Christ of Nazareth. We cannot continue doing whatever we feel like doing without regard to God's word and His Son, Jesus Christ, and this is called *self-will*. Humanity has been making and passing laws, and many of them are contrary to God's will, our heavenly Father, and His Son Jesus Christ. Many of us refuse to obey God through His written words with no concern about their accountability, but we hope that this book will open many eyes, those that are spiritually blind to the things of God. Many of us take no knowledge of God's commandments and His covenants. Humanity has been abusing the grace of God that He has given to Jesus Christ, His Son, for us. Under the Old Testament Law, when anyone transgresses the law, they can experience death right away, depending on the offense. But now we have Jesus Christ, who brings us the forgiveness of an immediate end; we take the grace of God to abuse His favor upon our lives. We are carnal-minded, and our ways are unacceptable unto the Lord our God, and we need to change.

### Isaiah 55:8-9

8. For my thoughts are not your thoughts, neither are your ways my ways, saith the LORD.

9. For as the heavens are higher than the earth, so are my ways higher than your ways, and my thoughts than your thoughts.

For too long now, we have misunderstood relationships and marriage the way God has planned it; instead, we have come to accept the idea of man, which is often contrary to God's will. Any time we refuse to obey God and allow Him to be the head of our lives, we are on our way to destruction because not too far away is the devil, who is waiting to devour you in his evil traps and deeds. Many of us recognized our errors and quickly made the necessary adjustment to correct our mistakes. However, many of us still refused to line up with the **Holy Spirit** so that He could help us to make our lives better. Remember this; God words will never change to please us because He said this,

### Psalm 119:89 (KJV)

For ever, O LORD, thy word is settled in heaven.

Many parents have failed their children in their relationship with their spouses. Many of us have cursed each other in front of our children, and we call each other nasty names. Some of us have an extramarital affair with another, and many times the children know of it. Because of this other person you have chosen to be a second wife or a sweetheart, you have violated the marital covenant between God and your spouse. You have invited problems into your life and home, considering the harmonious relationship you and your spouse have built for years or maybe with a friend will cause problems. Whatever promises you have made with that other person, go and ask for their forgiveness, cancel it, and renew your relationship or marriage. If not, your life will never be the same because of this extramarital affair, and remember, you will be living in sin. Take time out and reflect and consider; ask yourself what I am doing: Is it worth the stress?

When we enter into another relationship other than the person we started our life with, know that your life will never be the same because now there are two people to care for, physically, emotionally, and financially. Can you afford it, and if yes, is it the right thing to do? Please do not bring unnecessary stress to your marriage and home. Because of our sinful nature, we always want to please the fleshly desires and not God's Spirit. We began to cheat, unfaithful to the person we were only supposed to love; however, you would not like them to do the same to you. Is it fair?

When this happens, it will cause quarrels, many fights, and unhappiness, no more trust between both of you, and the children get caught up in their parent's tag and war. Soon something will give, and many times it is not pleasant. How many women must a man have to be satisfied? Again, how many men must a woman have before she is satisfied? Please remember that while we indulge in our selfish desires, the children will be part of the family's uncertain collapse.

Something came to mind as I was thinking how many of us men are so unfair to women and young ladies, even though some men do not care because they are not interested in a long term relationship; instead, they just want to get what they want and then fly away like a bird. Some men don't mind having as many intimate lady friends, but their girlfriend or wife cannot do the same. And again, many husbands don't worry about having extra ladies here and there, but they would not like their wives to do the same. Some husbands have more than one wife, yet a husband would not tolerate his wife having another husband living in the same house in this exact scenario. Do you see how some men plant seeds of dishonesty, and when reaping time comes, we cannot handle the fruit of our labor? Let us follow the word of God for our lives and marry one woman and make her your queen for the rest of our life. Wives, you go ahead and do the same, make that one man your husband treat him like an earthly prince and live with him in peace until.

When too many people are involved in an intimate relationship, no longer does that man/husband have the time to spend quality time with his family; he will have to share his time in two or more different places. Some marriages and relationships are experiencing terror because drugs and alcohol have become a necessary evil in their home; there is no peace. In a house with all of these negative things going on, what do you think? Haven't you come to your senses that your ungodly behaviors will affect your child/children's lives? That's why many are so unruly and disrespectful to you as the parents. However, it is still not an excuse for any child/children to disrespect their parents no matter what the circumstances may be, because you, the child, or children will have to give an account to God for your behavior towards your parents.

The scripture said this about children,

### Ephesians 6:2-3 (KJV)

[2] Honour thy father and mother; (which is the first commandment with promise;)

[3] That it may be well with thee, and thou mayest live long on the earth.

Husbands and wives, the love you have for each other initially at the beginning, if you have lost it? Go and find it again and put life into it. Is it old and not working? Go and restore it in Jesus' name. If you gave your love away to another, and when you come to your senses and want to make things right again with your spouse, be careful how you break up with the other person because it can get messy. Be satisfied with the person that you have and make something beautiful again. Love and consideration for each other are fundamental so that the *perfect will* of God be done in your family's lives as He has planned it to be on earth. Whatever the husbands or the wives must do, let love come back into the relationship or marriage again so that peace will reign in your lives and home.

Husbands and wives, and all those in a relationship, know this: there will be hurts, pains, disappointments, discouragement, hills and valleys, and possible potholes, and many other things in your life. Still, when they come your way, the decision that you make will determine the outcome, whether good or bad, or whether you are victorious or not.

Again, as we have said, this book is not about the writers; instead, it is about God and His only begotten Son, Jesus Christ of Nazareth, and their truth for the lives of humanity. This book will help society change their behaviors if they are teachable, and for their eyes to be open by the Spirit of God, they will come to see God's truth in His holy word, the Bible.

Furthermore, many thanks to everyone who has taken the time to purchase this book; we pray that you share the information with others. May God bless you and your family richly in Jesus's precious name.


Pastor Denburk Gregory
and
Minister Veronica Gregory

# CHAPTER TWO

Please understand the true meaning of love and the value of relationships and marriage because many of us do not value the next person. Therefore, from now on, parents, teach your children what God expected from them so that they can pass it on to their children, and let their children pass it on to their children and the next generations, that there is one God manifested in three persons. Namely God the Father, Jesus Christ the Son of God, and the Holy Spirit. Humanity needs to know about God the Father, Jesus Christ, the Son, and the Holy Spirit how important they are to us in our lives, and without them, there would be none of us. Therefore, we must line up with the Spirit of God in this manner, Spirit, body, and soul, so that He can help us to please God and God's Son Jesus with our bodies and lives.

Love is not and will never be the true meaning of sex, and sex will never be the true meaning of love. These two are two separate things, yet they are connected. One is physical, and the other is spiritual. Therefore, sex is a physical act between a man and a woman fulfilling God's will spiritually as He has ordained it in heaven. Therefore, according to the scriptures, sex is between a man and a woman when they are married.

Love is spiritual; love is not something you can see because it is spiritual, yet the manifestation of love can be touched, seen, and felt.

God has an excellent reason why He plans it that way. When a man and a woman get married, the husband should never need to go out of the marriage to seek sexual fulfillment because he has his own wife to satisfy his sexual desire. The same goes for the wife; she should never seek her sexual needs out of the marriage because she has her own husband. Unfortunately, some men desire to have sex with a woman before marriage to know what she will be in bed and the same about some women. We are not fruit in the market places, where some people taste somethings before buying it. Your action is sinful and will always be immoral, according to the scripture.

Also, when both spouses keep themselves for each other, there will be no place for the devil to come in and spoil the relationship. When both keep themself for each other, it will prevent sexually transmitted diseases (STD) and any other contracted diseases through sexual intercourse because they have kept themselves for each other.

Giving out condoms to school children, or any form of contraception, as I once heard, to prevent unwanted pregnancy and transmitting sexual diseases to any other person or group is not the answer. The response from the Lord is this, wait until you are married, keep yourself for your wife or husband to be; before that, it should not. Have you, the giver, considered that you are encouraging them to sin against their body and the almighty God which art in heaven. Having sexual intercourse with someone, that is not your husband or wife, is committing fornication, and it is a sin. Do you have no fear of God? You, the ones in authority, are supposed to know better and work to fix problems so that God will bless our cities, counties, States, and Nations; instead, we are passing laws to sin against the almighty God, who art in heaven. God sees, and He knows all that we are doing, and one day all of us who have sinned against the Lord God will have to give account for the things that we have done, whether good or bad.

Many men and women have used sex to destroy and spoil young girls and ladies after they have accomplished their evil deeds, then those guilty ones throw them to the curb to be devoured by wolves. Sex is used in the workplace to achieve several different things, such as to get a better pay rate, promotions, and to get favor on the job; all of these and more madness in the workplace that many of us do are ungodly behaviors. Let us remember that our body is the Temple of the Holy Spirit, and we do have a responsibility in taking care of that which is God's. Yes, our body belongs to God. He made it, and not we made ourselves.

Because of sexual greed through the lust of the flesh, many men are raping young girls and women and destroying their lives emotionally, psychologically, and physically. Some of these females get pregnant, and some abort the pregnancy, which also causes more problems in their beautiful lives. The women and young girls who were violated by the people who harvest wickedness in their hearts and committed sin against God and His Son Jesus Christ are guilty. You, the perpetrators, will not be guiltless before God because He will judge each of us in righteousness who sin against Him.

If you should die in your sin, you will be sentenced to life imprisonment without any chance of parole because where you are going; no human being has the key except Jesus Christ. Jesus can help you while you are alive, but He cannot help you when you die in your sins. If you only reach out to Him and ask the Lord to heal your mind and cleanse your heart, He will. Therefore, we can see that sex is not the foundation of love, but evil people use it for destruction. Sex is a benefit of love in a relationship, and it is not to be abused; instead, cherish it. As human beings, we should genuinely love a person of the opposite sex without any attachment of sex or money, a sincere friendship, don't you know how to do that. Loving a person is not sex, and it can never be because many of us humans misuse the purpose that God has intended it to be.

Because of those wicked men and young boys, they have put those females in danger of the possibility of contracting STDs if they, the workers of destruction, have diseases within their bodies; all of these acts are from the pit of hell. Surrender your heart to Jesus, and He will change your life before the time of too late.

The sad thing about this evil act of sexual abuse when the person/s who committed this violation gets caught, some of them are not adequately charged according to the law as it is written. Why? Because they or their parents are well known in society as the big and mighty, and they have connection and influence to people in high places, also, they are financially stable. Because of money and status, many people think they can destroy other people's lives and get away with it, but you will not, according to the Lord God universal law. Some may think that everything is okay because we are free or get away with those evil things on earth, but we are not free from our actions in heaven. Still, we have forgotten one thing, the righteous God, He, the righteous Judge, the One who sees and hears all of our activities; He will judge us in His time to come, and now is the time because He is very near. About the adult abusing women on the job, if you are married, would you like some other man to do this to your wife or fiancé or daughter/s? Please stop your foolish acts of your doings, and change your ways by repenting to God for your sins and so that you can live in Jesus' name.

Many ladies and young girls get pregnant for their sexual partners, and when this happens, they report to the person responsible for their present condition; some of the young men or gentlemen responsible for the pregnancy denied it because they don't want to face their responsibilities, or maybe they do not want their secret to be known. It was such a wonderful moment when you enjoyed each other, having a fun time of your life, but it comes with responsibilities to you, men and ladies. After the fun and enjoyment of each other, have you considered that you may get pregnant? If you are pregnant, do you have a job, or are you financially able to take care of the child when the baby is born? If you are not financially able to care for your newborn child, what are your plans? Are both of you mentally, physically, and financially capable of caring for your child? Do you have a place that you will now live, or do you plan to stay at your parent's house? Please remember, it is not about a newborn child for a few months; it is years; as a matter of fact, it is until the child graduate from college. Having children is a great responsibility; therefore, do not get into something you are not ready for now.

Getting pregnant at a tender age is not the best thing to do, young men and ladies, especially if you do not have a job, a place to bring mother and child to, and support help from others because your life will not be the same as usual. You will need child care when you need to go to work, or if you are still in school, you will need someone to stay with that child or put that baby in daycare; it takes money, and it can be costly. That is why you must be financially ready. That is why the Lord God has established marriage for a couple who is married to each other, and they should be mentally, physically, and financially ready for the family that will come. Do not get into a relationship and marriage if you don't know who you are because you will become a problem for yourself and your spouse or friend. Age is not maturity; instead, it is your ability to make sound decisions and carry them out responsibly.

With your baby developing in her womb, instead of facing your responsibility, men, and taking ownership of the pregnancy you have caused, you are now running away as if someone is chasing you. Stop and turn around and come back and face your responsibility. Being pregnant is a good thing to happen to any woman; however, there is a suitable time for this; as mentioned earlier, you need to be stable for the responsibilities that come with being a family. Ladies, forgive those men who have broken your heart in pieces by leaving you hanging like clothing on the line, do not store them up in your heart with unforgiveness because the Lord God expects us to forgive those that hurt, abuse, and neglected you and your family. Release those men and whomever they may be and move on with your life. Remember what the Lord Jesus said in His word that you must forgive so that your Father in heaven will forgive you when you do wrong. Many young ladies or girls that get pregnant face an uncertain situation because many do not have good family support to help them until they get back on their feet again. I am not sure, but this could be why many of them choose to have an abortion. At the same time, they are destroying a life that is within their womb. Whether you are married or unmarried, God knows about this pregnancy. He does not want you to abort that child that is developing in the womb. It is good to live a good life with others because we never know the person we hate today may be the one Jesus will use to help us tomorrow.

Parents, we know that your child has done wrong and brought disgrace into your home, but let us calm down and think about the best thing to do. Some parents never know about their child's pregnancy because they have aborted to hide what they have done in secret. But abortion is not the answer; doing the will of God is the answer. Sexual intercourse is supposed to be with your spouse. The process of removing the baby that is inside of the womb can result in future complications for later pregnancy; however, not all. Many married couples, both male and female, who are cheating on their spouse and hiding the affair, which results in pregnancy, recommend abortion. How many abortions will you continue to do to hide your shame or cover up the matter from your spouse's wife or husband? Is it worth it? Young girls and ladies, please do not allow your body to dictate what you need to do; instead, command your body to obey you in Jesus' name. Also, this could be the only pregnancy for you and no other, but you kill the only child that God has given you.

Please understand us; we have carefully examined this because we believe that those young girls' lives need to be preserved for their future. After all, their bright future is ahead of them to accomplish many things, no matter who is at fault, considering they are victims of circumstances. We are not against the principle of good home training; neither are we telling anyone how to run their home; it is not our right to do so. Nevertheless, sometimes we rush to judgment without considering the destruction awaiting her or anyone else if you should send her out from the house in anger by making hasty decisions.

A good relationship must have positive and healthy communication to stay alive instead of dying prematurely. A wonderful marriage needs honesty, politeness, and humility so that peace will be in the home. Spouses should never talk down to each other, especially before the children. Please do not call your husband or male friend a dog, as many women do. Did you marry a dog or fall in love with a person? Sometimes, a person's behavior may be like unto a specific animal characteristic, but a human is a human being as God made us. An animal is in the animal species. Without good communication in a marriage, there will be a breakdown in the relationship. It will be like going shopping and seeing the manikins dress up like a person, yet you cannot communicate with them, but this is for now, but soon, because of advanced technology. It is the same in a relationship or marriage without communication. It is the same with our children; the parents need to stop the shouting (yelling) and plan time to spend with them and communicate well so that you and your children can understand each other much better. Spend quality time with them and find out what is going on in their lives so that you can help them much better, especially in these problematic areas when it comes to being sexually active or being pressured by young men.

When our girl child gets pregnant out of wedlock while they live in their parent's home, let us not be too hasty to throw them out from the house because when we do such, we are sending them into the hands of wolves and dogs to eat them alive, meaning, people's behavior and character. Yes, she has brought shame to your family, no question about that, but we must still treat this situation very carefully; if not, it can get worse. But where will they go? I know that she is, or maybe living in a Christian home, remember she is your flesh and blood. Yes, you did not grow her up to fall into this temptation, but it happens; let us deal with this matter wisely. Let us have a conversation before anger sets in and causes destruction. We are not looking for excuses for what happens to young girls that are still living at home. What about our boys that are getting young girls pregnant? Why aren't we throwing them out from home too?

Please do not compare your family situation with your friends or neighbors; your home is yours, and theirs is theirs. By the way, do you know what is going on in their home when the sun goes down?

Many of these girls or young ladies did not make the right choice because they have allowed some males to pressure them into making the wrong decisions by enabling them to have sexual intercourse with them. ***Stand your ground if you are not ready for what they are asking you to do. Suppose they say that you do not love them because if you did love them, you would allow them to do what they are asking you to do. Be bold; tell them that they should not force or press you to do something you are not yet ready for or comfortable doing with them. If they genuinely love you, they should respect your decision and wait until marriage. Why does it always have to be about sex and not love?***

Some men by nature have a sweet mouth, maybe not all, but in general, many of us men used these sweet lyrics to melt females' hearts. Some men do this, and it is getting to know you, ladies, better to build a friendship. Men's communication with women or females can go two ways. One is to get her into bed, the other is to develop a relationship with her to win your heart to be his wife when the time comes, but first, it must develop into a healthy relationship. There must always be positive communication that should result in people understanding each other as time goes on. During this time, both males and females will come to know each other's likes and dislikes. Also, this is when both of you will get knowledge of each other and learn if you are compatible for a healthy relationship. Also, each other will see what they need to see in the other and discuss the dislikes and likes with a healthy compromise. So please, take your time to know one another before getting into marriage.

Do not make your fleshly desires or love cause you to be blind, and you overlook crucial things, negative behaviors, or characteristics of the person that may cause you pain and sorrows in the marriage later on. Sometimes it does not take too long in the union; as soon as the ring gets on the finger legally, then that which you saw, and you think they will change after marriage, you sentence yourself to a life of headaches, pains, and sorrows, just because of one-sided love. Many men use their sweet lyrics to entice women and young girls to sleep with them, and for many men, this is a game. Men, do you forget that there are still sexually transmitted diseases out there that you can contract, and then when you get it, you bring it home to your girlfriend or wife and ladies to your boyfriend or husband. The only remedy is to follow God's recipe, surrendering your life to Jesus Christ, live a holy life and self-control of sexual greed, and whatever else it may be that is having control over your heart and mind.

Yes, we plan to have fun and to have our way with these innocent females, but when it comes to sex, it is certainly not a game. Sex is a beautiful and exciting thing between a man and a woman, made by the Lord. It is a spiritual and physical act because the Lord God and His Son Jesus Christ establish this function within our bodies for their divine purposes. According to the scripture, when a man and a woman have sexual intercourse, they become one person spiritually, and that person supposes to be the husband and wife. The sinful nature in human beings aligns itself with Satan's characteristics, and those characters are rebellious against God, our heavenly Father, and His Son Jesus Christ, which art in heaven.

Therefore, we fail to follow God's commandments and covenants. We do whatever we feel like doing, not knowing we are still responsible for our actions to God. They are the ones who enable our human reproductive system to function to propagate, which is to replenish the earth and to enjoy each other as a couple in love. During our game, it produces fruit, and the seed that is sown results in pregnancy. Are we men ready to take care of our responsibility and nurture that child when that child is born? Will she be a statistic of another abandoned pregnant lady? Some men have not done the right thing towards the mother of their children in time past; we need to ask them to forgive us for how we have treated them in the past; it is imperative to forgive one another according to the scriptures.

God has made us, and the way He made us, we do develop feelings for the opposite sex, and there is nothing wrong with that; this is how the Creator God made us, and we cannot change it, but He did not tell us to go about sinning against Him by breaking His commandments **Romans 6:14.** Most of us make statements such as it's my body; I can do whatever I want with it; you are so wrong. But, again, it is my life, and I can do whatever I choose to do with my life; furthermore, you are wrong with your way of thinking and statement. Our body belongs to God, so is our life. God, the LORD has given all of us the will to choose, but there is an accountability that comes with the choices that we all make, whether it is good or bad, and all human beings will have to give an account to God for the free options that we have made.

While we were having a fun time with the ladies, she got pregnant, and many of us left her all alone in the cold to bear this responsibility by herself. We would not like any male to do this to our sister/s; why do it to somebody's sister/s or daughters? Because of the pregnancy, many men and young men do not want to face up to their responsibilities; they disown knowing her and deny the pregnancy. Some men encourage their pregnant lady to abort the pregnancy without respect for the innocent baby growing inside the mother's womb and the risk that comes with some abortion procedure. Remember that pregnancy is a child or person in the womb; they may not form as a recognizable person yet, regardless of how many of us think whether it is a person or not, know that pregnancy is a living person says the Lord God, **Jeremiah 3:5.** Many may not agree, but who are we to disagree with the living God if God says so. Many of us live a contrary life, and that is not the life that the Lord plan for humanity; instead, He the Lord God and His Son Jesus Christ has planned out a wonderful life for us, **Jeremiah 29:11** that is the perfect plan of God for all humanity. However, we go about doing what we want to do because of sin without regard for others.

Young people who are still living in their parent's house, please have respect for your parents, they are your father and mother, and because of who they are to you, you must respect them, and even when you are not living with them, you must continue to show respect. They may not be right in every aspect of their decisions or discussion, but because they are your parents, you must still have respect for them regardless of how they may treat you. Parents, we too need to know how to speak to our children in love, not because we are the parent, give us the right to maltreat them and be disrespectful at will. The ungodly lifestyle that many of us have chosen to live on the earth is not what our heavenly Father has planned for our families because our choice will result in death. Before us, there are two roads, life, and death; please let us choose life and live for eternity with Jesus.

Also, when you respect your parents, you follow the home rules, and by doing so, you please God the Lord and Jesus Christ. Rules are the foundation to maintain the integrity and stability of a peaceful and prosperous family. A home whose builder makes Jesus their foundation will face storms, trials, persecutions, and more because Jesus is your Rock of Ages and the enemy want you to lose faith in the Lord. Therefore, children, do not be quick to fight against your parent's home standards or rules; it is for your good. When these two areas are no longer sustainable, integrity and stability, we will see a family of confusion and unhappiness. When stressed people are living together, soon the home can become toxic. Please pray for peace to be in your home.

There is something that all men need to know about women, ladies, and young girls; this does not affect the wife or someone pregnant and has a roof over their heads. Men, whenever your wife or girlfriend is pregnant, we men do not have anything much to concern about because we are not the one who is pregnant. But the females in three categories, wives, ladies, and young girls, are the ones who are carrying around another person inside of them. Men do not have much to be concerned about because they do not carry around a big responsibility in their belly, but their pregnant wife or girlfriend does until she gives birth. Wherever she goes, the child is with her; that is why they need to be treated with care and respect. Come the day of delivery, men we can only imagine but the pain that she goes through only she and the Lord know. When a mother remembers the pain and suffering that she went through while she was pregnant with her child/ren, and when that child or they grows up, some of them are so disrespectful to their mother, this is wickedness children. Even though we have heard of cases that some husband has morning sickness, just like a pregnant woman goes through, sorry, but it happens.

We art to love them. We need to respect them. Being pregnant is not as easy as many of us men think. It is tough and challenging to carry a pregnancy for nine months, and at the time of birth, the anguish of the pain is so much, we men need to love and respect them for doing what they have done. And some women have early difficulty with their pregnancy, being sick so often, and constant doctor's visits. So again, we say it is not as easy as we may think; let all men show kindness and help as often as needed.

The Lord allows females to experience the incredible miracle by carrying a human being inside of her belly in a sack of water is indeed a miracle. We commend all females who sometimes want to give up but hold on, knowing that it will be over soon, despite the morning sickness, loss of appetite, weight gain, many changes in the body, yet not all. However, pregnancy has caused her internal system to function differently, and sometimes they react differently. Some ladies developed some health problems that can be life-threatening, and she deserves a gold medal. God is very great to see a woman sustain life within her and then bring forth a child into this world, a son or daughter, and for some, its sons and daughters. **"Congratulations, Mother's,"** and giving thanks to the only true and living **God, His Praise.**

**Yes, parents,** we know that you did not train your child/ren to be a loose child, but something happens to our child/ren by them making the wrong decisions that become a hindrance in their lives, and depending upon the mistakes it can change their lives for a very long time. Nevertheless, we make mistakes, depending on our approach to resolving the errors or mistakes can determine the outcome. Fixing something in anger is not the best thing to do because we make mistakes upon existing problems, and it can even worsen than before; please calm down?

Always pray about the situation or conditions that confronted you and your family because God knows all about it. He knows how it started, and He knows how it will end depending on your choice to resolve the situation that confronted you and your family. Because you put God first and seek Him for help in obedience to His directions, Jesus will aid you, but you must be patient with Him because the Lord God does not work like you want Him to. Therefore, listen to Him for the answers when you ask of Him; He will come through, but be prayerful, obedient, and wait patiently on the Lord.

Parents, if your girl child should get pregnant while living at home, instead of punishing her, why don't you call her and have an open and honest dialogue with her so that you will know exactly what has happened and what to do, pray for wisdom in this situation. Do not confront her in anger because you may push her away from you; also, the problem will worsen. She is also hurting because she gets pregnant without being married and in her parent's home. When you are ready to have that parent and daughter talk, please be calm and be a good listener, not too much of a talker, but listen to her as she explains.

After your daughter explains, find out if there is anything else you, the parent/s, need to know from her. After your daughter has finished explaining to you, it is your time to express your feelings to her about this unplanned pregnancy. Parents, please calm down and be honest to your daughter, speak to her in love and let her know how you feel about the unplanned pregnancy but remember, do it in love. Ask her who is responsible for the pregnancy. If you, the parent/s, do not know about the young man's family that got your daughter pregnant, now is the time to get all the necessary information so that you, the parents, can plan a visit. Find out what the family is like if she knows because many young pregnant girls do not know enough about the young man's family that she loves all this time. What type of family does the young man come from, and what type of person is he? You need to know this because you, the parents, need to take the next step to bring things together peaceable.

After explaining what the family is like, including the person who got her pregnant, get as much information as possible because you must visit the home. You, the parent/s, need to make an appointment to see the parent/s of the young man, or maybe it is an older person who put your daughter in the family way as it is sometimes called. Not doubting your daughter, but to verify that he knows about the pregnancy and what the next step needs to be because it is the right thing to do. Forget about abortion; it does not solve what has happened, and parent/s do not encourage your daughter to have an abortion to remove the shame from your home; it can complicate many things not yet known.

Be careful of abortion; the pregnancy could be the only one she may ever have and no more. God knows about our tomorrow and the future, but we don't know anything unless He reveals them to us. Maybe it is to plan a wedding even though they may be young, we don't know, it is your family, and you must know the best direction to go from here. Sometimes, we force marriage because of pregnancy, and our children's lives have been sentenced to hell on earth for the rest of their life. Please let us all make wise decisions because many lives have been destroyed already; let us not continue doing wrong based upon our directives. Choose wisely, our daughters, the man that will be your husband, and the ones that you mistakenly sleep with and get pregnant. It is not all about pregnancy, but our girls should keep themselves for their husbands and not abuse their bodies before marriage. Many of us could not wait for marriage when we were younger, and we have made many mistakes, and some of those mistakes are still with us up to now, but the Lord God is greater than our problems or errors. Ask the Lord God to forgive you for your past mistakes and reach out to those you have offended and seek forgiveness because forgiveness is so important to take that guilt off your mind.

Before visiting the parents of the young man who got your daughter pregnant, pray before going to his parent's home because the world we live in seems to be like a different world altogether because of the heart of humanity. Our heart is very deceitful above all things and desperately wicked according to God's word in **Jeremiah 17:9,** therefore, be peaceful and humble yourself. Because of the social status, some parents think that their boy child is too good for your girl child because you are not in their class, that's what some say, but the Lord did not say so. This vanity calls money, and it has caused many people to be very foolish and treat many who are not in their class disrespectfully according to their thinking by looking down on them as if they are nothing. They may deny the pregnancy for their son, not the son, but the parents of the son deny the pregnancy for him, and they were not there when their son was doing what he did to cause your daughter to be in the family way.

It does not happen in all cases, but in some, it should not happen at all, but because of the sinful nature within us, we always want to do things that are not correct regardless of whom it may damage. Because of some humans' selfishness, many of us use social status and financial stability to tear and destroy young girls' lives just because they are not like your family of wealth, you don't want them in your family, yet she is with a child for your son. Being wealthy should not give you the right to look down on others or on those who may be poor, and the middle class as humans like to attach names and class to people; it is not working; please stop it. I am not against anyone being wealthy and affluent, not at all, but we don't need to treat others as if they are not human beings. There is a place in heaven for the poor and needy; let us love them and treat them respectfully; however, you must accept Jesus Christ as Lord and Savior to get there.

People of the earth, we have the same enemy; his name is Satan; let us live in love and learn to love each other and pursue peace among humanity, and put the Devil to shame. Your son got a young girl pregnant? Don't you care for the tears, the embarrassment that you put that child through? Is it right? Because you know that you would not like anyone to treat you and your family that way. Often, the young man will deny the pregnancy because he is not ready to be a father, but do we remember the life of that young girl or lady? Doesn't her life mean something, too, like yours? He denied knowing her or having anything to do with your daughter through fear, but it is okay; thank the Lord God for science; something called a DNA test will verify if your daughter speaks the truth or the young man is lying at the appropriate time.

We know that some of you did not train your daughter in this manner, but it has happened. Parents sit down and talk about what to do, and please do not wait until pregnancy; we, the parents, need to teach our children about sex, not when it happens, but before it happens. Then invite your daughter to discuss the decision that both of you, "mother and father," come up with to fix what has broken. Keeping her at home is good because if you throw her out from your home, what will become of her? Too many children's lives have been destroyed already, so let us stop the destruction that awaits them by the enemy. But if you choose to keep her at home, please do not harass her, your daughter, with her mistake. What do we mean? Any little misunderstanding, the first thing that some parent's do, is to remind their daughter of their error that she got herself into; this is not good, please do not do this, because whether you want to believe it or not, you are killing her silently without knowing. Our children will make mistakes, but let us correct them in love and pray for them always to change.

Many of our children are looking for something they seek at home; however, because the parents are so busy achieving for themselves and their family, it sometimes causes communication breakdown. Our children go out in the world looking for something, but they cannot see it or what they need is already at home. Parents give them love and attention before the devil does it for you because you will lose them at that time. Parents are too busy working to pay the bills and make sure there is a roof over the family head, food on the table, clothing on their back, mortgage or rent, vehicle insurance, and so much more. Children, you need to be more sensitive to your parent's feelings and busy schedules because it is all for you and your future; therefore, please have patience with them. We know what you need, a good relationship, a bonding to learn love, kindness, compassion, honesty, humbleness, and so much more. Parents, find some time for your children before you lose them to crime, gangs, cults because evil surrounds them daily.

Everything that we are pursuing in this life for our comfort so that we will be comfortable are all vanities, and at the end of our life on earth, we did not make it into heaven. Being financially healthy for our future is an excellent thing, yet many of us forget the most important thing, and that is our dying soul on its way to hell. Our Lord and Savior Jesus Christ want us to slow down a little and reflect on our lives because where will your spirit and soul be at the end of everything? Will you be with your Lord or into outer darkness? Our home is crumbling in front of our eyes, yet we cannot see it because some of us are heavenly-minded and yet have no earthly good. Please do not get us wrong, but there needs to be a good balance between heaven, "spiritual," and earthy, "natural or physical," we need Jesus in our lives so that we can see clearly out of our eyes; because many of us are blind. We cannot hear from God or man because of the lust that dominates social media, and it has sucked many of us into its web and world of madness like a vacuum. Let us invite the Lord God and His Son Jesus Christ in our ups and downs, and there will be a difference? Have you forgotten that the Lord careth for you? The same thing happens in our spiritual life, is the same in our physical life, too busy to spend quality time reading the Bible and spending quality time with our God, our heavenly Father.

Sincerely bring all of your troubles and problems to God who careth for you, and as you wait for your breakthrough, you will see that the Lord is a gracious God that answereth prayer. So, while the Lord is working on your behalf, read His word, fast and pray, be patient and live a good life, and watch God how He will come through for you and your family in the precious name of Jesus.

We know that every household is different, and every family member has a distinct personality of expression. Nevertheless, even though we live in this vast earth that we call home, each household supposes to experience love, joy, peace, and success in their life according to the commandments that we have received from the Lord God and His Son Jesus Christ through the Holy Spirit.

We, humanity, according to the scriptures, have trained animals to obey us, birds, beasts, and many other things, yet we cannot tame our tongue and obey Jesus. However, when it comes to obeying God, the Creator of heaven and earth, who also created the visible and invisible things, we find it hard to follow His commandments. Many of us human beings rather obey each other rather than to obey God. What? **Matthew 10:28,** Don't we fear Him who can destroy both body and soul? God's commandments are not hideous; the Lord's burden is not heavy at all. These are the two greatest commandments that are given to us, and if we obey them, we will have eternal life as we accept Jesus Christ as our Lord and Savior. Please study who your neighbors are; it is imperative to our well-being on this earth so that we will reign with Christ Jesus for eternity. **Deuteronomy 6:5, Matthew22:37-40, Mark 12:31-34, Luke 10: 25-37.** The Lord Jesus Christ reminds us, Christians, through the word of God, how to love the brethren, but many of us have failed Bible test in how to love our neighbors who are not yet of faith in God. We better learn how to love one another on this earth because, without love in your heart for humanity, you will not make it in because the Lord God knows our hearts. I hope that we are ready to meet the Mighty God of justice who will judge us in His righteousness on that great and terrible day of the Lord.

There are some situations and conditions that we find ourselves in, but no one's experience is the same, and not everyone responds to their experience in the same manner as others. Therefore, we must help those who need our help to overcome the dire situations they find themselves in. For all those going through a bad relationship, a marriage with many regrets, financial disaster, or whatever it may be that you are experiencing, please do not allow your present situation or condition to cause you to go into depression? Remember that your current needs are a test and not your future; don't allow your situations to determine your future. Learn from it or them and strengthen yourself for a brighter tomorrow and a victorious end. Again, please do not allow your current predicament to dictate to you what your tomorrow will be. God is in control of your tomorrow, but will you let Him? There is a bright future ahead of you, but only God knows about it; therefore, consult Him to give you an insight into your journey towards your destiny.

Whatever anyone of us does, please do not allow depression to come upon you? Depression is a terrible sickness or disease and will destroy your life. Depression is not from the Lord but from the devil who works upon your mind. According to the scripture, paraphrasing, **St. John 10:10,** Satan comes to steal your mind to control your heart; after he gets to your heart, he plays with it and sows the seed of evil and wickedness, and the result is for your destruction. The word of God informed us of the intent of Satan; therefore, when the pressure of life becomes too much to handle, and you feel like your mind is breaking into pieces, call on Jesus, who comes to give you life and life abundantly. Many people have gone through this battle and recovered, but many never recovered from the fear of life that has locked them up into Satan's prison, and only God can deliver and heal them. Therefore, let us pray that the Lord will unlock those prison doors of the mind and lose those who are in Satan's prison in Jesus's name.

Therefore, when we go through a bad relationship, be very careful of handling the situation or any problems; seek the Peace Maker who will give you peace during your storms. When the flood of life seems to be too much for you, call upon the God that dries up the Red Sea. When the devil put obstacles in your way to prevent you from crossing the River Jordan, call upon the God of Elijah and Elisha. When the Jericho wall stands in your way, preventing you from entering into your blessings, call on the God of Joshua. Finally, when Satan puts his shackles on your feet, call upon the Lord Jesus, who is a chain breaker, and when the enemy comes in like a flood to devour, call upon the Holy Spirit, who will raise a standard against them.

Many may think that they can get through life without the Lord, but we tell you that no one can get through life without God, whether you believe it or not, because the Lord God wakes us up every morning and gives us sleep at night. It is the Lord God who kept us in our sound mind. It is the Lord God who provides us with the strength to move around. There is nothing that we can do without the knowledge of God. He knows all of us before we were conceived in our mother's womb; therefore, let us take our problems to Jesus and ask Him to help us because He knows our thoughts before we speak. **St. John 15:5.**

The broken relationship He can fix it. Confusion in your mind; He can heal you. Marriage is going through stress heading for divorce, He the Lord God will fix it for you only if you are willing to allow Him to help you. Whatever it is, God is our answer. Throughout this book, the Lord's name will be mentioned many times because He is the Creator and giver of all lives. We must read the word of God that is found in the Holy Bible, but without being obedient to the will of God by surrendering your life to the Son of God, it means nothing.

Wealth and riches are good, but it is not eternal life? What is good health without eternal life? What is a successful life without eternal life? What does it matter to have a wonderful family and everything just as you desire them to be? Without Jesus Christ, you and I are nothing? It is not how you and I began our journey, but how we finish our life on earth is what matters. Many have started well, but in the end, they cannot be found in the book of life; this is called a wasted life? But many have started with not enough, much poverty, pain, suffering, hungry, sickness, afflictions, troubles on every side, but their faith and trust was and still is in God the Father of all creations, and they are found written in the book of life. Does this mean this is the way to live our lives? Oh no, but somehow, they that have little, their trust is in their God and always giving thanks and praises and living for Jesus.

If you have an ear to hear, all ye nations on the earth, listen to what the Spirit is saying to us. Love God, worship Him only and serve Him. And love your neighbor as you love yourself. God bless each of you dearly!

We hope that some of the information in this chapter will help you make better and sound decisions in your home and life in handling problems. Pray and learn to be a good listener, be patient, talk less, and be careful making hasty decisions in anger. And again, we say, pray about everything. Many thanks!

# CHAPTER THREE

## Instruction before Prayer

I know that we have already said it, but we will repeat it. In this book, we, the writers, will try to convey to you, the readers, as best as we can about relationships, marriage, and divorce. Because of our decisions in our marriage without considering the next person's feelings, we, the guilty ones, have caused so much hurt, so many pains, broken hearts, disruptive lives, and so much uncertainty. Many of us who have already divorced never put much work into it to save the marriage. Suppose we put as much effort into saving the marriage by keeping the vows we did when pursuing each other for a relationship. In that case, we are sure that many marriages could have been saved instead of ending up in divorce and broken lives.

Many people's lives have been destroyed because of divorce, especially those who have young children when the marriage was dissolved. After the divorce, some wives do not have the financial resources to establish themselves because some of them never work, and the husband has all the money, and sometimes they hide the money before the divorce. The small amount of money that she received may not be enough to take care of the children. Some couple does not even go through a divorce, but her husband abandons the family because of another woman, gentlemen God is watching our behavior, and it smells. Wives, are you praying for your husband and family daily from the temptations that surround them daily? Husband, are you praying for your wife and family daily from the enemy that lurks around them to devour? The outcome of the current condition depends upon that mother in her decision and the direction that she takes. All because some of us men abandoned her for another woman, they are now facing the uncertainty of life. Sometimes it is not the husband's fault because a woman can destroy her home in one day that has taken years to build. Please, ladies, learn how to tame your tongue because it has been getting many of you in trouble. **James 3: 2-12**

## The Storm

The pressure most times is on the females to care for their young ones when a relationship has broken, and the children become innocent victims. Husband and wife, you need to learn how to live with each other for the sake of the marriage and family, but most important, obey God and His Son Jesus Christ. During a divorce, some people's lives are like thunderstorms or hurricanes; the strong wind is the unpleasant words thrown at each other; the debris is the things that one or both uses to inflict pain upon the body. Sometimes emergency care is needed; sometimes, there are casualties. Gentlemen and ladies, this cannot be from God. By now, both of you should have known that Satan, the enemy, has infiltrated your relationship or marriage for the sole purpose of destroying you and yours'. Resist him, Satan, and all of his workers of iniquity according to the bible,

### James 4:6 (KJV)

7 Submit yourselves therefore to God. Resist the devil, and he will flee from you.

Husband, wife, and children "family" are riding out the storm of life, and it is not pleasant for any one of them; as you pray for your family, please remember others who are experiencing hardship and harsh life on this earth. Some husbands and their wives' lives have been turned upside down as the storm of life racked them back and forth during the stormy wind of their life that blows upon them during their quarrels, and it affected the children. They fight, court appointments, maybe alcohol and drugs are involved, which some people refer to as hell on the earth. The destruction that the storm and the hurricane left behind is devastated. So is life in families experiencing such an ordeal in their home because they have allowed Satan to use them as an instrument of destruction against each other because we did not resist the devil. The enemy comes into our lives and homes like a strong storm or as a tornado to kill and destroy.

After the terrible experience that many people have gone through, which they did not plan for or foreseen. The storm blew through their lives and resulted in divorce or separation. However, it is not over for many because it bothered their minds severely; after a while, they had mental and psychological problems because they could not handle them. Undoubtedly this is not the Lord's doing; instead, it is of Satan, the devil.

Sometimes it is hard for many to start all over again; however, our recommendation to you is Jesus Christ, He is The Peacemaker, and He is a loving Savior. So many tears have fallen to the ground; thank God, He has seen those innocent tears, and the guilty will not go unpunished. Many have lost so much financially, many disappointments, self-blaming, condemnation, guilt, mind wandering, evil thoughts, death, and so many more ungodly things. Please remember, spouses; it is not all about you and you; remember the innocent children who will be affected permanently and some for a short period; nevertheless, there will be pain that someone will experience. All these things that come upon the human race and many more have affected our lives because we yielded our free will to Satan's works and devils and not to the will of God.

Let us not get into marriage because you may feel left out and want to be like your friends or family members. Please do not follow family and friends if you are not ready to be a groom or bride. Please do not let anyone force you into marriage if you know that you are not **Mentally, Psychologically, Physically, Emotionally,** and

**Financially Stable.** Marriage is not a game to see who plays the best match or who will win or lose. Marriage is sanctified by the Lord God in heaven and not man. Humanity carries out the ceremony to fulfill God's will that has already been established in heaven.

Everything that our God does, He did it first in the spiritual realm because He is Spirit. And everything that humanity does is done in the physical because we are earthy. The spiritual things of the Lord are manifested in the earth physically. And everything that humanity does, we do it physically, and then it is converted into spiritual action. Therefore, when a man and a woman get married, they become one flesh according to the scriptures, and by that, the will of God has been fulfilled on earth as the Lord ordained it to be in heaven. As we carry out God's will on earth, it becomes accomplished in the spiritual realm in heaven by God and not man, and heaven and earth are in agreement.

Therefore, let us position ourselves and wait on the Lord for that woman and for that man, and He will guide you to the person He has for you. This advice is for the women, not because the man looks handsome with a golden smile, his tooth is polished, and they are correctly aligned; it does not mean he is the one for you; wait on the Lord and let Him. Not because he may be rich or have lots of money, a big house or many houses drive a nice car and are verse educationally, that doesn't mean that he is the one for you. These are good things that a man needs to acquire to take care of you, his fiancé, to be his wife and his children to come. He may be rich with materialistic things but lacking in love. His house may be filled with the beautiful things of this world, and yet his heart may be empty with pure love and compassion for you. But what we need in a person that will be a husband or wife, a boyfriend or girlfriend, is a person that exemplifies the fruit of the Spirit *(Galatians 5:22 – 23)*. Wait on God and let Him guide you to that person. Some of you ladies rush into marriage and never get to know the person well before being wed, and later on into the marriage; you are experiencing hell on earth; the same also goes for many men.

When you see someone you love, gentlemen and ladies do not make the worldly things that they possess be the main focus. Instead, make love be the centerpiece because love will see you through the rough times that may come. Love each other truthfully, honestly, and faithfully to please the Lord Jesus. The lies may come when you do that, but the relationship or marriage will stand the storm. When money fails, love keeps you together, even if things should get rough in your life. Love God, self, and each other with understanding, and He will keep you together even when the drought of life confronts you from the enemies.

Not because a man speaks beautiful words into your ears and you feel an electrical wave moving within you, he may say the right word, but did he mean it. Even the devil used the serpent to speak great words into Eve's ears, but the devils were found out to be a liar and a deceiver. These are just a few ideas you need to know before getting into a relationship and then marriage.

Please, always pray to God, who art in heaven, for your spouse. But, unfortunately, because some of us are too hasty or impulsive and eager for marriage, many of us make the wrong choice and live with a person who does not truly love you.

Some ladies possess unique facial beauty and a lovely body, and these two qualities have drawn some men towards them and not for their personality or character. Now it has become a sexual attraction, yet there is emptiness because there is no love. After they have achieved their devilish game, not all, yet it is many, women have been used, and they are left hanging like clothing on a line; this is not of the Lord; instead, it is of the devil. Isn't this behavior just like Satan? Remember that Satan comes to steal, kill, and destroy. Men, let us not be an instrument of Satan, the devil, instead let us be a vessel of honor unto our God in heaven. Men don't want to be used by any woman, yet we have no godly fear of using them and dumping them as if it is a game; shame on us, please let us stop this behavior.

If we would stop being so anxious and take our time to access things around us, about others, we would be able to see many things clearly and people for who they are. When we fail to seek our Father in heaven and wait upon Him for the answer, we get ourselves into a relationship that has become a disease in our lives. Sometimes they start well but become bad later on; that's why we have to continue praying for each other. Please get godly counsel before marriage! Godly counsel is often given, but the Adamic nature, which is the sinful act to be rebellious, awakens within us, and that sinful nature shows off itself, and you will see a person for who they are. Many of us allowed the devil, Satan, to use us to be a destructive force upon each other to destroy lives. Satan does not care for you; he is a user and a manipulator just to get what he wants, and what he wants is for all humanity to die in their sins.

Please turn your life over to Jesus Christ of Nazareth, and you will come to know that He is a very loving Savior, and He will not treat you like Satan, the devil. Our heavenly Father, yes, the One in heaven, wants the very best for all of us, but we must listen to Him and obey Him, by His word and through His word in Jesus's name. So let us stop running down fortune and fame because all those things are just vanities.

Husbands, it is our responsibility to pray for our wives and children. It is also the wife's responsibility to pray for her husband and family in Jesus' name.

Please, we encourage you to get a Bible and read it every day so that the Lord can speak to you through His Word, and at the same time, you will become knowledgeable in the word of God. It is always good to know the word for yourself, what the Lord is telling you through His written words. Why? Because there have been many deceivers out there who are Satan agents and are giving false interpretations about the Lord God for their selfish gain to deceive you.

It is vitally important that each of us have a personal relationship with the only true and living God that there is in the entire Universe. Our heavenly Father loves all of us dearly. He loves us so, so much that He sent His Only Begotten Son, **Jesus,** to die for all of us. Therefore, the Lord God is the **Only God** we must obey, for there is no other God other than our Father in heaven. So, as we read **The Holy Bible,** we will come to the knowledge that God has a perfect plan to save all of us and for us to live a productive life on this earth in Jesus's name.

As you read this book, you will see that the writing is lined up with the word of God. This writing does not flow as many others because we write as the Spirit puts information within our spirit. We are not just writing to make money, but rather that you will be knowledgeable about the word of God concerning marriage and relationships. You may not be aware of this, but the devil is attacking families' by perverting the true meaning of what marriage is supposed to be, and he wants to destroy the union by attacking the husband or the wife. Sometimes he will use the children to accomplish his evil goal. No matter what devices the enemy uses, let us come to that knowledge of his instruments of destruction and let us resist him in Jesus' name.

Do not always rely on someone's words because of their popularity in society, especially when writing about spiritual things; make sure the writings line up with God's holy word. Because there are times, it seems that we do have a vast difference in the interpretation of God's word when too many people interpret the same scripture or verses in so many unusual ways it can be confusing to the unlearned. It can become confusing, and that is not what the Lord wants. Therefore, each of us needs to seek the Spirit of God to get the revelation of the mystery of God's written words, which is in ink and paper. When the writer writes a religious or spiritual book, they must always line up according to God and His Son Jesus Christ's written word. There is much money in writing spiritual books and singing songs, but let us do it for the Lord to help others and not for our selfishness.

Please, we ask of you, the readers, to read the word of God for yourself, get a **Bible Dictionary** or a **Strong Concordance Bible Dictionary** so that you can understand God's word better because of the languages that they speak back then, and the true meaning of those words. These languages were **Hebrew, Greek** during the Old Testament times, and those languages were still in the days of the Lord Jesus, including the **Latin Vulgate** during Jesus' time on earth. We live in a world where many deceitful people are perverting words to tell what they want it to be and not what it is supposed to be. So much corruption in this world to please ourselves! Good becomes bad nowadays, and evil becomes good; the Lord Jesus Christ is coming soon. Can't you see how people are becoming so wicked each day, and evil manifests itself in the heart of many people?

All of us need to get the correct understanding and the correct interpretations of God's word so that we will not be deceived at any time. We cannot continue living in darkness and ignorance; there should be no excuses. We must read the word of God and allow the Spirit of God to help us with the revelation of the mystery of God.

Marriage was and still is of the Lord God Almighty; despite what many may say about marriage negatively, marriage is always the right thing to do. It is never God's will for anyone to live together and call themselves husband and wife without being married. Marriage will be discussed in more detail in another chapter, but for now, continue reading and enjoy.

Bible says,

**Romans 3:4 (KJV)**

4 God forbid: yea, let God be true, but every man a liar; as it is written, That thou mightest be justified in thy sayings, and mightest overcome when thou art judged.

## *Now it is time for us to Pray*
## **Prayer of Binding**

Our Father, who art in heaven, hallowed **"ho*ly*"** be thy name. (we/I) come to you in the mighty name of Jesus Christ; I repent of my sins in Jesus' name. Lord, forgive me and cleanse me with the precious blood of Jesus. Father, I forgive those who have offended me and abused me wrongfully in Jesus' name. Father God, I pray that all those I have offended will find it in their hearts to forgive me in Jesus' name. Father God, I Worship You. I honor You and Adore You. Lord, You are from everlasting to everlasting, and there is no other besides thee.

Father God, cover my wife/husband, our children with the blood of Jesus, cleanse their heart and mind from all unrighteousness and forgive them for all the wrong they have done in Jesus' name. Father God saves the children from sin in Jesus' name.

Father God, your word said that ***whatsoever I bind on earth that You will bound them in heaven, and whatsoever I loose on earth, they will be loosed in heaven by You.*** Therefore, dear LORD, hear this prayer and answer (me/us) speedily in Jesus's name.

### **Matthew 16:19 (KJV)**

[19] And I will give unto thee the keys of the kingdom of heaven: and whatsoever thou shalt bind on earth shall be bound in heaven: and whatsoever thou shalt loose on earth shall be loosed in heaven.

### **Matthew 18:18 (KJV)**

[18] Verily I say unto you, Whatsoever ye shall bind on earth shall be bound in heaven: and whatsoever ye shall loose on earth shall be loosed in heaven.

1. Father God closed every door that I have left open, the doors that the enemy uses to enter into my life and home in Jesus' name.

2. Father God closed every door that my wife and I may have left open that causes the devil to come in and destroy our marriage in Jesus' name.

3. Father God closed every door that the children have left open to the devil to cause problems in their lives in Jesus' name.

4. I bind every controlling spirit that is controlling the mind of our children in Jesus' name.

5. I bind every confusing spirit that is controlling my wife/ husband's / children's lives and our marriage in Jesus' name.

6. I bind every generational spirit of diseases, sickness, illness, diabetes, cancer, migraine headache, high blood pressure, blood disease in the mighty name of Jesus.

7. I bind every spirit of limitation that causes me not to progress in Jesus' name.

8. I cancel every evil plan that the enemy has planned against me in Jesus' name.

9. I cancel every curse that my enemy has spoken over my life/ wife/ children in Jesus' name.

10. I cancel every tongue that wishes my family and myself premature death in Jesus' name.

11. I cancel every mouth that wishes my marriage to be broken in Jesus' name.

12. I cancel any thought of divorce between my wife/husband/children and me/ in Jesus' name.

13. I cancel every spoken word that wishes my children to fail in life in Jesus' name.

14. I bind every destiny-killing spirit in the mighty name of Jesus.

15. Father God rendered every evil spirit powerless in my life/wife/husband/children in Jesus' name.

16. I command every spirit of darkness to come out of my house in the mighty name of Jesus.

17. I command every tormenting spirit tormenting me/ my wife/my husband/our children in the mighty name of Jesus.

18. I bind every manipulating spirit in the mighty name of Jesus.

19. I bind every unclean spirit that is showing itself in my dream in the mighty name of Jesus.

20. I bind every spirit of rape, destruction, theft, home invasion, fear, and premature death from my home in the mighty name of Jesus.

21. I bind and cancel every spirit of lust in the name of Jesus.

22. I command the red sea that prevents me from moving forward to dry up in the mighty name of Jesus.

23. I break down the Jericho wall that is standing in my way in the mighty name of Jesus.

24. I command the Jericho wall to fall to the ground in the children's life Jesus' name.

25. I bind every unclean spirit, and I command you to come out of my house/wife/husband/children in the mighty name of Jesus.

26. I bind the spirits of limitation in my life/husband/wife/children in the mighty name of Jesus.

27. I bind the spirit of sexual perversion from my family in the mighty name of Jesus.

28. I bind and cancel the spirit of rape from over our children in the mighty name of Jesus. Holy Ghost fire burns up and destroys their works in the precious name of Jesus.

29. I bind the spirit of jealous eyes in my marriage/on the job/our children's educational achievements in the mighty name of Jesus.

30. In the mighty name of Jesus Christ of Nazareth, Father God let every spirit of darkness scattered from around my family and me in Jesus' name.

31. Lord Jesus, cover my family and I with your blood so that monitoring spirits cannot see us and monitor our movements.

32. Father God cancels every activity of evil spirit in my family's lives and mine in the name of Jesus.

33. Father God, let the Holy Ghost fire surrounds my family and me each moment of the day in the name of Jesus.

34. Father God, I bind and cancel every spirit that would cause my wife/children's pregnancy to be miscarriage through jealousy in the mighty name of Jesus.

35. Father God, I bind and cancel every spirit of confusion that others have sent to break up my marriage in the mighty name of Jesus.

## Prayer of Loosing

Father God, your word said that whatsoever we loose on earth, that You will loosed them in heaven. Therefore Lord, according to Your word, let it come to pass in Jesus' name.

1. I loose myself from the captivity of the devil in the mighty name of Jesus.

2. I loose my wife/husband/children/grandchildren from the captivity of the devil in the mighty name of Jesus.

3. Father God, pour out Your blessings upon my life/wife/husband/children that the enemy has hindered in the name of Jesus.

4. I loose the mind of our children from the devil's control in the mighty name of Jesus.

5. I command the devil to loose (my prosperity, house/ job/ mind/children/home in the mighty name of Jesus.

6. In the mighty name of Jesus, I loose my destiny and my calling that the enemy has hindered, which causes a delay.

7. In the name of Jesus, I break down every Jericho wall that is standing in my way.

8. In the name of Jesus, I cancel and loose myself from every satanic covenant that I have made consciously or unconsciously.

9. In the name of Jesus, I cancel and loose myself from every blood covenant that I have entered into.

10. Oh God, destroy every evil activity in the lives of my family and I in the mighty name of Jesus.

11. I renounce, denounce, and loose myself from every satanic and cultic covenant from my fore-parents, which has become a generational curse in my life/wife/husband/children in the mighty name of Jesus.

12. Holy Ghost, burn off with your fire and destroys every demonic residue, germs, and bacteria from out of my body and off my body in the mighty name of Jesus.

13. Father in the mighty name of Jesus, everything that I have eaten or drink that will harm me and cause bad health, oh God, cause me to pass it out so that I can be loose.

14. Father God, according to Your word, *No weapon that forms against me shall prosper, and every tongue that rises against me shall be condemned in judgment in the mighty name of Jesus.*

15. Father God, I release your peace that passeth all understanding into my home/life/upon my wife/husband and children and their family in Jesus' name.

16. Oh God, deliver my family and I from the entrapment of the enemies in the name of Jesus.

17. Father God, I cancel any form of premature birth of my baby that is in my wife's womb from the plan of the devil in the name of Jesus.

18. Father God, I loose my wife's womb from the devil, and I ask dear Lord that you will bless her womb to bring forth children in the mighty name of Jesus.

19. In the name of Jesus, Father God, I lose our children wherever the enemies have them tied up.

20. Father God, open the prison doors that our children have got locked up in by the enemy, and let them be loose in Jesus's mighty name.

21. Oh, dear God, let us Your people who are called by Your name, be prosperous in Jesus' name.

22. Father God remembers the homeless in their conditions; heal their mind in the name of Jesus.

23. Father God, we ask that You will remember the fatherless and the motherless in the mighty name of Jesus. Father God, fight for them; many of them have no food to eat. No proper place to stay. Many have been abused and misused. Please stand up for them, and help them before it is too late in Jesus' name.

24. Father God, I lose my in-laws from the stronghold of the devil in the mighty name of Jesus.

25. Father God, I disengage myself from all works of the devil that others have brought upon me through ignorance in Jesus' name.

# CHAPTER FOUR

Greetings to all believers in the precious name of Jesus Christ of Nazareth, and unto all the unbelievers who one day will become our brothers and sisters, we greet each of you in the mighty name of Jesus Christ Savior of the world. We ask each of you for your patience as you read this book. We encourage you, the readers, to get a Bible to verify if what is written in this book agrees or aligns with the word of God. No matter how you may feel or refuse to accept the truth from God, know this, it is never God's will for any married couple "male and female" to get a divorce or to be separated from each other. However, the selfish and fleshly desires within us had caused many to break the covenant of God and the covenant we made when we got married and said, yes, I do. How easily we forget the excitement that we once had, the love that each other expressed to one another.

My darling, how easily have you forgotten the promises and dreams that we have discussed and the plans for the future; what happens, sweetheart? Remember that we promise each other that we will be there for one another, knowing that the day of marriage is drawing near. What has happened since we got married? It seems that you are not the same person that I got married to, is this you? My darling, why are you speaking to me in such a manner? I remember the sweet words that my ears used to hear. Was that to get me, or was it truly love from the heart? You used to be gentle, but now, you are so harsh to me? If there is something that I have done to you, my darling, not knowing, please forgive me? Honey, your silence is killing me slowly.

Sweetheart, please do not accuse me of something that I know nothing about and call me names that you will regret ever speaking against me falsely? And even so, baby, why call me such nasty names? Remember I am your wife?

*Many of us have spent so much money to have a wedding that you and others will remember for a very long time to come. But it is sad to say that many marriages have not lived long at all! Many marriages died too quickly; no one was willing to resuscitate life back into the relationship. The bride desires a glamorous wedding, expensive rings, clothing, food, the place for the reception, baking cakes, and so much more. Let's not forget all the wedding gifts and the expensive gown.*

*Especially on the actual day, no one wants to be late (except for some brides who think that if the man loves her, he should wait patiently for her). The bride was so excited that her day was near; rejoicing and gladness filled the air. All the well wishes, gifts, the stress, and we can go on and on. Some of our couple's honeymoon experience was not good, and many the bitter-moon. It is so sad to say, yet it is the truth about some marriages.*

Nevertheless, we thank our God for all those couples who have taken time to labor to see that their marriage works. Many may say it wasn't hard for them in their relationship and marriage, but for most of us, it is hard work to live with someone who makes themselves to be complicated. Again, we say that marriage is not just that one-day event, but it is a lifetime of commitment continuously working on it to work out. Just like we take our vehicle for preventive maintenance before going on a long trip, we are supposed to do preventative care in our marriage so that nothing suddenly breaks apart. In many marriages, it is so toxic that they result in violence. Ask God for some patience, and ask Him to take away the anger inside your heart. Oh yes, it is not easy to live with some people after the wedding day, because for some reason they change suddenly not for the better, but the worse. We need Jesus Christ in our lives so that we can live a life of peace. We need Jesus Christ in our marriage so that it does not break. Like a binding substance that keeps things together, that is the value of Jesus Christ in our lives; therefore, invite Him into your life and home.

It was never and will never be God's perfect plan for mankind to hurt each other by breaking up a relationship or in any other way. The Lord knows that it caused pain to the couple and the family when they separated themselves from each other. The hurts and disappointment that each other have, yet they cannot compromise to make it work; instead, they blame one another for the stress in the relationship. Once again, couples, please remember the innocent children that get caught up in your tag and war. Is it fair? Wait just one minute to all the couples that are having problems in their marriage? Parents, have you honestly considered the children in all this mess and madness that both of you have caused? Husband and wife, male and female friends, you have caused yourselves pain, suffering, agony, financial stress, and some of us developed mental and psychological problems over relationship disaster.

What have they done to deserve the pain and hurt that they (the children) will have to experience? The mockery that many selfish friends and others will mock them concerning both of you. Their emotions and the sleepless nights! Maybe some of them may become suicidal. Cutting themselves because they fell abandoned. Turn to drinking and smoking. "Bad relationship results in a bad home, and bad home results in a bad life, sometimes affecting their ability to make sound life decisions."

From the beginning, God's perfect plan for humanity was that a man and a woman would make a home and have children, and both would raise them together. But as we know, in this world full of sin, it does not always happen the way God has planned it for us, and it is all because of the decisions we have chosen to make. So let all of us ask the Lord our God to forgive us for not following His plan for our lives, and let us move on for a better tomorrow and future in Jesus' name.

We will explain to you what the Lord God expects from all of us. But we need to obey Him, the Lord, in every area of our lives. God loves us, and He wants the very best for all of us, but we must obey Him and do whatever he asks of us.

**We need to look at two areas for a moment, and these are the areas, Toxic and healthy.**

Some people in relationships are not experiencing a healthy and stable relationship throughout this earth, their relationship is toxic. And when something is contaminated, it is poisonous. It is no longer suitable for consumption because it will cause diseases, sickness, or even death. Also, a toxic environment is not healthy for any person to live in or to be nearby. Spoiled food will kill you or damage you seriously; a toxic environment can kill you or damage everything around it.

Many relationships are dead, yet it is alive through force or denial. Something dead does not have life in it; in this case, someone in an unhealthy relationship is on a ventilator waiting, hoping for a miracle. There is hope, my friend, and this situation can be changed if you desire change in your life, but this is only by Jesus Christ of Nazareth.

Let us examine when a person drinks too much alcohol and gets drunk. Drinking too much alcohol on a dinner date or even at home can cause a person to vomit and mess up their clothing, maybe in the area where they were or somewhere else, disgrace themself and have side effects. When this is done away from home by yourself, the authority can ticket you or arrest you because you have taken too much alcohol. It was too much at one given period for you to drive, you can cause injury and even death, and too much drinking for an extended period can destroy your liver and so much more.

It is the same thing when a person is living in a toxic relationship. The home environment gets polluted with hate and bitterness, anger and unhappiness, fussing and fighting all the time. When a man or woman, husband or wife, starts arguing constantly, they get high, like when someone gets high on alcohol or drugs.

When a couple starts to fistfight or throw things at each other, at that time, the relationship is no longer stable or suitable to live in; it is like a volcano waiting to erupt.

It is a shame and disgrace when a Christian home is toxic. When the husband raises his hand and hit his wife or throws her out of the house, even some unsaved family gets it right when many Christian homes are getting it wrong, when we are the ones that should be teaching them how to live and have a healthy relationship with their spouse.

Many people like to give this excuse that they are not perfect, well, so does that gives you or anyone the reason to hurt another person? Even so, yes, before God, we are not yet perfect to God's **standard of perfection;** well, why don't we seek Him and get to be perfect? This is one of the reasons why Jesus came to earth from God our Father, who is in heaven for us to be perfect as Adam and Eve were at the beginning in the garden of Eden. Jesus died for all of us; therefore, we owed Him everything because He shed His precious blood on the cross at Calvary so that we can become perfect in Him.

Some marriages that have become toxic end up in divorce, and others end up in death at the hands of Satan's instruments. Some end up with mental stress, and others end up with regrets. Some toxic marriages and relationships end up with lifetime paralysis, lifetime disfigurement, all of those, and more are of Satan, the devil. Therefore, repent unto God in Jesus' name, and make your life worth living on earth.

A healthy relationship displays love in every aspect of the word love to their spouse. None of the spouses must declare that the relationship is a fifty-fifty relationship, but rather, it must be one hundred percent on each side. Even when things may not always be correct, however, because of God's love within their hearts, they will display the fruit of the **Spirit Galatians 5:22-23** in their lives and home; also, they will bring this God's love to their workplace. A healthy relationship must have love as the center of the union; love will also consider the next person's needs in caring and always remembering others' feelings. Love causes you to care for others than yourself. True love will cause you to go out of your way "Sacrifice," making sure that all the necessities for the house are taken care of for a healthy relationship. Such things as food in the house, the bills being paid, helping out with the children, "men," assisting in the kitchen to prepare food for the family, laundry, ironing if possible, and so much more. These things remove stress from the home when each spouse works together as a unit.

Sometimes in marriages, it may be that the relationship experiences stress because of the spouse and the girlfriend or male friend. When a load-bearing post and beam compromise its strength because of substandard material or the weight on them is more than they were specified to carry, after a while, they will fail because it did not meet the building specification. So is it with relationships between the husband and wife or any form of relationship? Suppose the connection between the man and woman is not built on a proper foundation, and the foundation is love; it can fail. In that case, the relationship will experience stress, and too much pressure causes friction. The marriage or relationship will experience failure or burn-up because of the stress that someone or both causes to happen. Love is the center post and the beams resting upon the foundation of all relationships, and then some of these friendships become fruitful and turn out into marriages. Less not forget that the outpost of a house is significant for the stability of the house's strength. Therefore, every relationship and marriage must have good steel bean or wood posts to help strengthen marriages. Remember that love is the foundation, and all the other parts are the support structures that keep love alive.

***Would you mind using the following words as a worksheet? Fill in the lines with the characteristic behavioral pattern that make your marriage with your spouse successful.***

Love________________________________________________

Joy________________________________________________

Peace________________________________________________

Longsuffering________________________________________

Gentleness__________________________________________

Goodness____________________________________________

Faith________________________________________________

Meekness____________________________________________

Temperance__________________________________________

Compromise__________________________________________

When you identify the source, what next? You need to handle the situation at the right time and in a suitable place. Be always polite when addressing a problem of any sort in the home or even at work because too many negative words and aggression can cause you not to accomplish your goal. Be frank, get to the point, and do not force an answer, be patient. Most important, before you conduct any form of meeting or fact-finding, pray to God for **knowledge, wisdom**, and **understanding** because you will need them to be effective in your speech. Do not forget that you also need the ***Spirit of discernment*** to discern what has happened or will be happening right before your eyes.

Husbands and wives, we must put our sinful nature to death. What is that? It is the heart of humanity, the will to sin or be rebellious against God. The soul of humankind is corrupted because of sin. The soul is the intellectual part within you that causes you to reason; it is humanity's will. The soul and the spirit of humanity will never die, and these two need to be subject to the Spirit of God; that's why we cannot live without Jesus in our lives. There is a war going on, and the battle is the mind and the Spirit within us; they are contrary to each other because the soul of man wants to please itself, which is not pleasing to the Lord Jesus. Because of the sinful nature that all human beings inherited from Adam, we are subjected to sin against the Lord God and His Son Jesus Christ at any time. With the sinful nature within us, we always find ourselves doing the opposite of what God expected from us; this is called rebellion. There is some exceptions for those who surrender their lives completely over to the Lord Jesus Christ, The Savior of the World. Even then, we need Him daily to help us to do the right things that please our Father in heaven because when we think this is right, it may be wrong. We are reminded in the scripture that we need to mortify the flesh daily; else, we will find ourselves sinning against God, our Father, and His Son Christ Jesus. When we yield to our own will, the result can be devastated.

Let all of us resist the temptation of the devil because when we resist him, he has no other choice than to flee in Jesus' name. Sin should not have dominion over anyone of us, the children of God; instead, let the righteousness of the Lord be our portion.

### James 4:7 (KJV)

*⁷ Submit yourselves therefore to God. Resist the devil, and he will flee from you.*

### Romans 6:14 (KJV)

*¹⁴ For sin shall not have dominion over you: for ye are not under the law, but under grace.*

Marriage is sacred and honorable. Our God, the Lord, is the First Person and the only One who has established this great institution between a man and a woman. The Lord God has planned humanity's lives from the beginning of time, how we art to live and please Him as a single person and a couple when we get married, meaning a man and a woman to each other. "All other marriage is not and will never be recognized by the holy God and His Son Jesus Christ." When a person in authority performs the marriage ceremony on earth, God's will is fulfilled on earth as He had ordained it in heaven; in this case, they are now legal to complete the oneness of being joined together after the ceremony at home to consummate the marriage. They two are now one before the Lord, complete or perfect because of the matrimony.

When it comes to humanity, the LORD, our GOD, through Jesus Christ, created the spirit and soul of mankind first, and then He made the flesh of humanity out of the dust of the ground according to the scriptures in *Genesis 1:27, 2:7*. According to the Bible, when God made man's body, He made the only man and woman, yet at that time, the woman was in the man Adam, but not yet manifested in the flesh to be seen like Adam. God is a good God. He is Awesome in everything that He does. Only Adam could be seen in the flesh at first, yet Eve, his wife, was in him, ready to be taken out in God's precious time. The human race came from these two people that the Lord God by His Son Jesus Christ created and made since they are the first two people as human beings on earth, all human beings inherited from him the sinful nature. The sinful nature is to rebel against God, always the opposite of the truth.

To all the nations of the earth, know this for sure, it is your responsibility to know who God is and that He is the greatest throughout the entire **UNIVERSE** and ever will be. There is none like Him and never will be. He is a good God. God is so wonderful and caring for all of His children; His children are the human race. At the appointing time that He has outlined in His **Wisdom**, at that appointed time, He the Lord took a rib out of Adam, "first surgery" by doing so, the Lord God uses that rib that He took from Adam and made a woman. And this is how the woman came to be in the manifestation of the flesh. Humanity has nothing to do with creating anything that there is; it is all the LORD our God doings. God is the only one supposed to be credited for this vast Universe and all that there is, **visible** and **invisible.** There are absolutely no big bang events that ever happen; if it did happen, God would be a liar like us human beings, and He is not a man that He should and can lie. When we believe such foolishness, we rob God of His glory and praise, and it should not be like that at any time.

Since the Lord is responsible for creating us, knowing the precious time that He has taken to make all of us, in His image and after His likeness, we owned Him all the glory and praise. Again, according to the scripture, He created them male and female, Amen. When a man marries a woman, they become one again when Eve was in Adam. And this is how the Lord God brings man and woman back together, which can only happen through marriage between a man and a woman. This is how the Lord plans it, and there is no other way despite what some people who are an instrument of Satan perverting the institution of God's divine plan for humanity. And that is the only method that our God has put in place for the human race concerning marriage. Therefore, society needs to accept God's will concerning marriage because it is what it is, and there is nothing that we as human beings can do to override God's perfect will.

Marriage is supposed to be when two people, a man, and a woman, develop a relationship with each other and decide to marry or tie the knot as it is sometimes called *(and if the word knot is proper to be used, who is untying our knots.)* Marriage on the earth between man and woman fulfills God's perfect will that He has already established in heaven. The whole purpose is to replenish the earth and to share affection in the marriage. The word **"replenish"** means to **"fill** or **fill again."** Therefore, it should be clear to us as people on the earth with intelligence or those who are teachable what the Lord

God meant when He commanded Adam and Eve about replenishing the earth, and the perfect will of God is through marriage. But as we all know, that we have not gone the way God planned it. The sinful nature of humankind rebels against the true and living God, and we have children out of wedlock; this was not and still is not God's perfect plan for humanity. Also, so many lives have been destroyed not seeing the sunlight of God.

**Just a side note:** Husband, when you and your wife got married, where was she at the time of the ceremonial event? Answer if you can? Sure, at my side. Thank you so kindly for recognizing that! So why are there so many husbands having their wives somewhere else other than their side? So when the Lord our God made the woman, where did God have her? Yes, from Adam's rib, which is at his side, and that's where she needs to be for the rest of both lives.

Your spouse is not to be treated as if she has no value; she is the jewel that God gave you to be your helpmeet; therefore, please take care of your jewel. Don't put her behind you, where Satan the enemy can and will take her captive from you. She is the man's helpmeet, and that is direct from the Lord. The wife's responsibility is to support her husband in every area of his life to accomplish and succeed all that God ordained them to perform on the earth to fulfill His will.

To truly understand marriage, we must know of the person who created or established this institution. Marriage is sacred, and it is both spiritual and physical. The spiritual part of it is of the Lord God, and the physical aspect of it is by us mankind through the perfect will of the Lord. The Father of all creations is the One and only Supreme Being who is responsible for all the things we see in the sky, on the earth, and under the earth or wherever they may be seen. He is the **Creator** of everything by **His Son Jesus,** and without Him, there is absolutely nothing that would ever be in existence. This is the God who established marriage. He gives us guidelines on how to have a successful and peaceful relationship not to experience pain, hurt, and disappointment in marriage. However, when we fail to follow the marriage recipe from God, we will experience the areas mentioned above and more. So, let us reconsider and examine ourselves and see where we have gone wrong, and ask the Lord Jesus to help us to get back into the right relationship with Him and our spouse to fulfill His purpose in us.

Our Father in heaven wants us to get married, but when we do, He requires the husbands to love their wives as Christ His Son loved all of us and gave His life for us. Also, He directed the wife to honor (submit herself unto) her husband according to the scripture. Wives, your husband needs to know that you love him; however, what a man needs is your respect for him. When his wife respects him, she shows love and honor. Husband, your wife, does not require you to respect her the way you are going about it, but rather, what she needs is for you to truly love her and exemplify the characteristics of the true meaning of love. When you love your wife the way that God told you to love her, she, in turn, will be loved and respect you even though a person can respect you but does not love you. Also, some have love but no respect for their spouse. We all need to know the proper recipe for the relationship that we have between a man and a woman to work right so there will be no confusion.

It is like baking a cake; without the correct ingredients, it will be a cake, but it will not be delicious. It is the same with relationship and marriage; you and I cannot love the way love is supposed to be displayed without knowing what love is. If you and I do not have love within our hearts, we cannot give or show love to anyone. It is simple, how can we offer what we do not have. Can you give a person a dollar when you only have a dime?

A tree without roots will eventually die, so are relationships, and marriages without love will slowly die. Therefore, love is the principal object or center of every relationship and marriage. The absence of love produces hate. The absence of God is the devil, who is also named Satan. The absence of prayer is defeat. The absence of faith is fear. The lack of knowledge of God is confusion, little wisdom, and not much understanding of the Lord.

Men and women, young men and young ladies, let us be knowledgeable of love, and when we know the true meaning of love, let us cultivate love and practice it like a farmer who needs to have a good harvest from the crops he planted. To have a good harvest, first, the farmer must prepare the ground for the seeds or planting, then he needs to water that which he planted, and he will have to depend on the Lord to send rain to water his crops. Finally, he must maintain the crops by ensuring that nothing is growing with them that will choke or stifle his crops' growth because if he doesn't, he may not get a good yield. Therefore, a farmer does not just plant his crops and forget it; he must pay attention to his field.

It is the same with love and relationship; you must cultivate it by making sure no one comes into your love garden and pollutes it with hate, confusion, gossiping, lies, and so much more, and these are just some of the rotten fruit of the devil devises. If we ignore what is going on in our relationship with our husband/wife, one day suddenly, the husband may be bringing another woman into your home wife, or the wife may become pregnant for another man. Let us not be naïve, but let us be alert, pray without ceasing for each other. Husband, safeguard your home so that the devil does not enter your wife's home that you have tirelessly prepared for her and her family.

Business places and residential homes do have electronic security devices to protect their property from violators with an evil intention who allowed the devil to use them to break in and steal and then destroy both properties and lives. It is just the same, we the husband, need to make sure that God is our protector against the evil forces in the world, both spiritual and physical. Mostly Christians, the devil hates you and for what you stand for, the righteousness of Christ Jesus. Let all of us live a holy life unto our God because He said this in His word,

**Psalm 34:7 (KJV)**

*⁷ The angel of the LORD encampeth round about them
that fear him, and delivereth them.*

## God at work

### Genesis 1:26

*And God said, Let us make man in our image, after our
likeness; and let them have dominion over the fish of
the sea, and over the fowl of the air, and over the cattle,
and overall the earth, and over every creeping thing that
creepeth upon the earth.*

When the Lord God thought of us, male and female, in the mind of
God, He had already planned for all mankind's success on the earth,
which all of us human beings live in temporarily for now, in this
physical body. Our life on earth was supposed to be fabulous without
any pain, suffering, sorrow, hurts, and disappointments without sin.
But jealousy from our enemy, the devil, has robbed us from such life
intended by lying to Eve, and then it spread to all mankind because
Adam accepted that which he was commanded not to do. Yes, it was
Eve that he lied to, but that lie is still active in this present world
because many of us are still living a life of lies; why? Because not
all of us have yet lined up by accepting the Salvation plan that God
gave His Son Jesus Christ provided for us. Oh yes, Jesus came, and
He brings Salvation for all human beings; many have rejected this
grace from God through His Son Jesus, and they are now waiting
for everlasting punishment. You don't have to be like them; because
you are alive, and there is hope in Jesus.

Many have accepted the eternal life in Christ Jesus, and in Jesus
Christ alone is this life that many seek. Nevertheless, even now, so
many are refusing to accept Jesus Christ as their Lord and Savior.

If they die without the precious blood of Jesus cleansing them from unrighteousness and experiencing the New Birth, they also will have their place in hell, experiencing everlasting punishment. According to the scripture, refusing Jesus Christ, who has this eternal life, will bring forth death and destruction in the end, which is to be separated from God forever.

Nevertheless, it is not too late for us who are still alive to receive this wonderful life that He promises to all and to receive this life, you must accept Jesus Christ our Savior, the Son of God the Father. All we need to do is accept Jesus Christ as our personal Savior, and He will change us and make us a new person in Him. Thus, we will receive that everlasting life, never to die the second death as promised us forever. However, when we make Jesus Christ our Lord, it is not the end but the beginning. Why do I say this? Accepting Jesus Christ as Lord and Savior are not enough; it is the initial first step.

The second is to live our lives as Jesus told us in the scriptures. As Christians, we must live our lives according to God's written words, and His word can be found in this wonderful book of books called the Holy Bible. Yes, we are not yet perfect to the person who God the Father wants us to be; however, we thank God for His Holy Spirit, **Who** indwells within us throughout our lifetime on this earth. He, the **Holy Spirit,** will work in us so that there will be no spot or wrinkles in our life when Jesus Christ shall ascend from Heaven to receive God's children out of this present world, and all of us then will be perfect before God and His Son Jesus Christ of Nazareth. *Eph 5:27*

Please take notice; the Father said, let us; the word *us* is a plural pronoun. That means the Father could not be talking to himself, but rather, according to the interpretation of the scriptures, ' The God-head was present agreeing about humanity's existence. God did not just make us, but He planned us, He discusses how we should be created, and that is to be like Himself (His image and likeness.) We were to have dominion over everything that the Lord God has made on the earth. However, because of sin, we have lost that authority of power to rule over God's creation on the planet earth, but not to worry, Jesus came and gave it back to us, but we are not doing a good job operating in it.

The Lord, our God, made humanity to worship Him and Him alone because He is the only **God**, and besides Him, there is not another.

### Isaiah 43:10-11 (KJV)

*[10] Ye are my witnesses, saith the LORD, and my servant whom I have chosen: that ye may know and believe me, and understand that I am he: before me there was no God formed, neither shall there be after me.*

*[11] I, even I, am the LORD; and beside me there is no saviour.*

The LORD GOD is the **Creator** of the **Universe;** however, knowing the nature of some people, we sometimes are a people pleaser; therefore, we please them and ourselves and disobey our God. Many have come to worship other things that God creates, and those things are not God. Are we not old enough to know right from wrong? Or, isn't the Holy Spirit convicting our soul that which you are doing is wrong? Many of us subject ourselves to govern by another spirit instead of the Spirit of God. We are disclaiming God from being the **One** who is responsible for the creation of the world. Not everyone will accept the truth, but we pray that the Lord will open their eyes to see and their ears to hear; as the scripture said, ***"Those who have an ear to hear, let them hear what the Spirit saith."***

### Isaiah 42:5 (KJV)

*[5] Thus saith God the LORD, he that created the heavens, and stretched them out; he that spread forth the earth, and that which cometh out of it; he that giveth breath unto the people upon it, and spirit to them that walk therein:*

Therefore, God made man and woman to **replenish** the earth, and there is a proper way of doing such. According to the scripture, God has given us examples to follow, and these examples are in the Bible that a man and a woman should not be intimate until they are married to each other. Again, we choose to satisfy the flesh by breaking the law of God without any regard for the result or consequences that it may bring our way. Some parents have not taught their children about the Lord God, who rules the universe, and what He expects from us human beings. Many parents lack knowledge about the Lord; therefore, they cannot teach their children about God's law, and many more who are not learned in the things of the Lord do not know the righteousness of God; so they are set up to perish. Therefore, we art to teach and instruct them about God's law and His covenant and the consequences for not doing them.

Because of the lack of knowledge concerning the will of God, many of us ignorantly sin against God, but it is due time for us to train up our children in the fear of the LORD GOD the Almighty so that He will bless us and His righteousness will be our comfort and delight.

As many of us rightly know of this fact, so many people in this present world despise godly corrections, even in the church, and it is not good. Nevertheless, even if they refuse corrections, we must still offer it to them so that their blood won't be on our shoulders. God makes man and woman so that they will **replenish** the earth, but first thing first, man must marry the woman so that they both will be husband and wife before having babies; this is the **perfect** will of God for all humanity.

**Genesis 1:26-27** speaks about man and woman; the first created parts of mankind were our spirit and soul. We are spirit and soul. Humanity's spirit is within the body, and without the spirit, the body cannot live. When a person dies physically, their spirit leaves the body and goes back to God, who created the spirit and soul. The soul is our consciousness, the ability to reason, to know good and evil. However, it was never God's plan for anyone to experience death, but because of sin, influence by Satan, the Devil. His original name is Lucifer; he is no longer referred to as that name because of what he did. Eve was lied to by Satan through the serpent to deceive us so that we will disobey God, and every time we refuse to do what the Lord God commands us to do, we rebel against the Lord, which is a sin. And Satan is still busy working and carrying out his wicked plans, and he is working very hard to continue deceiving humanity by lying to them so that we can believe something else rather than the truth. And what are the lies? Anything contrary to the will of God the Father who is in heaven. When humanity lies, we take on Satan's characteristic, he is the one who told the first lie in this world, and the lies are to deceive humankind; therefore, when we lie, it is to deceive the person that is lied to for our selfish gain.

**John 8:44 (KJV)**

*⁴⁴ Ye are of your father the devil, and the lusts of your father ye will do. He was a murderer from the beginning, and abode not in the truth, because there is no truth in him. When he speaketh a lie, he speaketh of his own: for he is a liar, and the father of it.*

Because of sin, the body died and decayed, but our God the Creator has a glorious body for us, a body that will never experience death; if there is no death, there is no decay of the body. But we must accept Jesus Christ as our Lord and Savior, and to do so, we must repent of our sins and live for Him in righteousness and be holy as our Father in heaven is holy.

**Genesis 2:7** The Lord our God put the created man into the body that He made from the dust of the ground. Again, the spirit and soul of humanity were created by God through His Son Jesus, amen, and this truth is for all those who didn't know. Jesus is the One who created humanity and made everything that there is, and without Him, nothing is made that was made. And so many of us have come to hate him the creator; humanity's shame is ever before us. So, God made Man, Adam, and then He made Eve, Woman. After God made these two human beings, God gave the woman Eve to Adam the man; before any intimacy between Adam and Eve, The Father of humanity gave the woman to the man; they were legally married and were ready to have children. **Genesis 2:18-25** tells us what the Lord God did concerning man and woman.

**Genesis 2:15** *And the LORD God took the man, and put him in the garden of Eden to dress it and to keep it.*

God gave the man (Adam) the responsibility of taking care of the garden; he was to dress it by keeping whatever was in the garden looking good and proper, suitable to God's acceptance. Everything in the garden was Adam's responsibility, how they behave or conduct themselves; as a matter of fact, everything during that time before the deception was perfect. He was to make sure of what comes into the garden and what goes out of the garden. Adam allowed the enemy to enter the garden illegally and polluted the serpent's mind, and then used the snake to lie to Eve, which was his intention all the time, was to deceive her and to get to Adam, and Satan was successful. Satan plans to destroy humanity so that he may eliminate mankind from this world at any cost, and we allowed him to be successful in doing just that by being careless doing what we feel like doing.

Satan did not care about Eve; she was just the means to his end. His focus was not Eve; instead, his target was Adam. Satan's target was to get back at the Lord because he was upset. After all, God made humanity like Himself, and not Lucifer, who became Satan the Devil. There is nothing else spoken in the Bible that the Lord made in His image, other than us humans; therefore, we are unique to the Lord, which is why He died for us. Adam was the one to whom God gave the commandment, and if Satan could influence the woman, he knows that he will be successful in bringing the man down. Even now, this operation is an ongoing practice in this present world. How many women Satan has used to destroy man's life, but many of us men have not yet come to our senses, we are still falling for the same old trick by putting trust in human beings rather than God, even though many of us men are at fault to our own destruction.

The commandment was given to Adam; that's why sins did not activate until Adam take of the fruit. Eve first took it; nothing happened until Adam took of it. Even now, the Devil, which is Satan, is killing off the men on the earth. Where are the men? Many are in prison, not free to carry out God's work in His Kingdom, and many are doing the work of abomination. God planned our lives and ordained them to be; those plans are for God's purposes before creating the world, but sin came in and disrupted them. But there is a day coming that the Lord alone knows about in which He will put all things back together in Jesus's name. So many men and women are caught and locked up in their fleshly desire for death and destruction to come.

As we continue to read the scripture, in **Genesis Ch 2,** God commanded Adam not to eat the fruit in the midst of the garden because he would surely die if he did. However, in chapter three, Eve tells the serpent that neither should they touch it or eat it because they will surely die in the day that they do. However, the serpent came and told Eve that she should eat, and her eyes would be opened, which she did, and the door of death was open but not thoroughly until Adam took and ate of it. Whom do we listen to, God or the devil? Should we listen to mankind or God? Humanity will fail us, but God will never, never fail anyone of us.

Adam and Eve sin against God the Father by disobeying the Lord, and because they refused to obey, which is sin, all humanity after Adam was born in sin because we all came forth from Adam as the first man. In the beginning, since Adam and Eve were the first human beings made in the image and likeness of the Lord God and they sin, everyone since then was born in sin and inherited the sinful nature. They rebelled against their Creator, and death entered the human race. However, the loving and caring God made a way of delivering humanity from this death sentence by giving us Himself through His Son Jesus Christ. God manifests Himself in His Son, sending His Son Jesus to die for sinful humanity and to shed His blood for our forgiveness. Even now, we are still displaying this behavior, being contrary to the will of God the Father and His Son Jesus Christ. Mankind sin; therefore, it needs a man to fix what humanity broke, and what was broken is the relationship between God and humanity. Also, heaven and earth were no longer in alignment, sin has interrupted God's perfect plan for humanity, and this will need to be fixed. The Lord does not dwell in unrighteousness because He is a righteous God; therefore, heaven and earth are no longer in a perfect alignment as at the beginning when the Lord created heaven and the earth.

God's perfect connection with Adam was interrupted through disobedience, and one day the Lord will put everything back together in its perfect state as at the beginning.

Since we were born in sin, we become a slave to Satan because we start to do sinful things that are not of God, but our God has a plan to deliver us from Satan and sin, and this plan is to have His only begotten Son Jesus Christ to pay for our sins. The cost for our sins is so great that humanity cannot afford to pay for it themselves. Yes, there is a cost to purchase us from the slave master of sin, which is unrighteousness, to the righteousness of God; it will have to be paid with someone's life and not with money; yes, it will not be ours because we are tainted with sin. Only Jesus Christ alone, who has no sin, was born of a ***virgin woman*** named Mary. Jesus is the only One who can save us from the wrath to come.

Why is Jesus so special or different from us through conception? Good question! Jesus was not conceived in the womb of the ***Virgin*** Mary by any man like our earthly father's; instead, Jesus's Father is God like Adam was at the beginning. Therefore, God needs another man like Adam, one who would obey Him, so the Lord God put or place Jesus the Word into the womb of Mary. ***(Mary was a virgin*** *young woman, meaning she never had any sexual experience with any man before the birth of her first Son Jesus)* The Holy Ghost is the Spirit of the living God the Father, and Mary was conceived with child. Jesus' DNA is not from earthly man; instead, His DNA is from God, our heavenly Father.

When Adam was made from the dust of the ground, he was **perfect** in all sense of perfection until Satan, the devil, deceived him through his wife Eve. Therefore, because of the sinful nature that all humanity would inherit from Adam, our precious Lord Jesus could not come from man. So instead, God the Father gave His only Son to us by allowing the Holy Spirit to put Jesus who came from heaven into Mary's Womb and clothe this precious person with the flesh of man, and this is how Jesus is the Son of man, and at the same time, He is the Son of God.

Therefore, we could not pay for our sins by our self, because of Sin, instead, the Lord God needed someone who has no sin within himself, and this person is **Jesus.** Our blood is tainted with sin, but the blood of Jesus is **Pure** in every sense of **purity.** That is why we always call on Jesus to wash and cleanse us with His precious blood because water and soap cannot cleanse us from the filth of sin; only the blood of Jesus can do such and so much more. The blood of Jesus is so pure and free of any impurity that just the shedding of His blood on Calvary and only by His blood can we receive forgiveness of our sins from God the Father. Therefore, we must always have a forgiving heart for everyone so that peace will abide within us. Because we are forgiven for our sins by God, our Father, which art in heaven, it is expected of us to forgive others who may offend us?

In **Genesis 2:16-17,** the Lord God has given Adam a directive, and he understood the message because Eve, his wife, explained it to the serpent; therefore, we now know that both Adam and Eve knew what to do and what not to do. But the serpent's influence over Eve was too much for her, and she yielded to his directive. Therefore, let us not blame Eve; let us learn from her mistake because we are still doing the same thing. Didn't God command us to love our wives as His Son Jesus loves us? How many of us are following God's directive in this case? Didn't God command us to love our neighbors as we love our self? How many of us are genuinely following this directive? Didn't God command the wife to submit to their husband? How many have the spirit of submission to yield?


## *God consideration for man*

**Genesis 2:18**

Every living thing on the earth has a kind after their kind, but Adam has no one like himself. God has made this other person in His image, and after His likeness, too, it is time to unveil this person (Woman) we knew as Eve. Remember the scripture, **Genesis 1:26,** when the LORD God said, let us make man in our image, and after our likeness, when the Lord God created Adam, He also created a woman who we now know was Eve. When the Lord made Adam from the dust of the ground, Eve, his future wife, was also made at that time, but she was in him. However, the manifestation of Eve was not yet until the appointed time by the Lord; and at that specified time, the Lord took the rib and formed Eve.

Spiritually she was already created, but to see her was not as yet like unto Adam. God is so Wonderful and Great in whatever He does and will be doing. The Lord is the only and true God that we must listen to and obey because He has the whole world in His hands, and since He is the one who created all that there is, who knows of them more than God the LORD.

**Genesis 1:27 (KJV)**

*27 So God created man in his own image, in the image of God created he him; male and female created he them.*

Therefore, the woman was already created, her spirit and soul, but she did not yet have her own earthly body like her husband to be Adam. In man, the rib that God took from Adam was a woman, and the Lord shaped her into a person like Adam. Adam did not know, but God knew of this because He is the One who put her there; that is why at the right time, God went and took her out of Adam's side and finished up what He began from the beginning.

Men and women are extraordinary people on earth because we are God's masterpiece. God took Eve from out of the man, and through marriage, God causes her to go back from where she came, at the side of man. She is no longer in the man; she is now standing by the side of her husband, fulfilling God's plan for their lives, in this case, "marriage," making them be one again; therefore, God's will is done on earth as in heaven, and it is spiritual.

## *Side notes:*

Men and husbands notice very carefully where God took the woman from and where He God put woman again. She was given to her husband, Adam, to be his help-meet, meaning someone to be at his side helping him in every manner of his affair to complete the task God has given man to do in the earth. She is not a slave to any man or husband; neither is she your punching bag. You will find punching bags in the gym; that's where you need to go and do boxing. She is not to be abused at any time; she is supposed to be your princess and queen. She is not your gun target or practice instrument. She is not your baby factory machine. She is your wife, girlfriend, or fiancé, whomever she is to you, she must always be treated with true love and be respected and giving God thanks for giving her to you.

According to the scripture, her husband is to protect his wife since she is the weaker vessel. She must be loved as the scripture gives us the method of loving our wife, not when we need her in the bed, but at all times.

### 1 Peter 3:7 (KJV)

*⁷ Likewise, ye husbands, dwell with them according to knowledge, giving honour unto the wife, as unto the weaker vessel, and as being heirs together of the grace of life; that your prayers be not hindered.*

## *Side note:*

Husbands, please notice very carefully that our prayers can be hindered if we fail to treat our wives with love and respect as the word of God caution us to do His will.

### Ephesians 5:25 (KJV)

*²⁵ Husbands, love your wives, even as Christ also loved the church, and gave himself for it;*

We men must have a tender heart towards our wife; she's no less a person (human being) than men. She was made by the same God that made us, and she was given the same breath of life by the same God that gave us ours, so a man cannot be a woman; it is impossible. A woman cannot be a man; again, it is impossible; we are all different in our body chemistry makeup, this is how our heavenly Father chose to make us, and we should be satisfied with ourselves.

### Proverbs 31:10

*Who can find a virtuous woman? for her price is far above rubies.*

## *Notes:*

Wives, you also have your part to share, and when you align yourself in your position according to the scripture, everything will be well; it will stop any evil influences in the home with prayers. The scripture said wives,

### **Ephesians 5:22-23 (KJV)**

*[22] Wives, submit yourselves unto your own husbands, as unto the Lord.*

*[23] For the husband is the head of the wife, even as Christ is the head of the church: and he is the saviour of the body.*

## *Side notes:*

When wives respect their husband or male friend, you can win him over or his heart; why? Men love to be respected as a man and not to be treated like little children. We pray that this man who is your husband has been washed with the blood of the Lord Jesus Christ. We have heard that some Christian husbands treat their wives worse than some unsaved people; this art not to be so. Do you not remember that we represent Christ in the world, and whatever we do reflect His holy name in our behavior? To all those husbands, shame on you. You read the word; don't you have an understanding of what you read? Wives giving respect to your husband is not enough, but you must pray daily for your husband that the devil does not pollute his mind and corrupt your husband's heart and bring confusion in your life.

As human beings made in the image and after the likeness of the Lord God, we are now like the God-head, namely God the Father, Jesus Christ the Son, and the Holy Ghost; these three persons are one. We need to honor God and praise Him, and most importantly,

He is the only God that we humankind must bow down to and worship because He is the only true and living God. Yes, there are many other gods that many people worship, but there is none like unto the true and living God. If we should search the entire Universe, we cannot find another God like the God of Heaven and earth. Therefore, our daily duty as mankind "humanity" is to worship God and give Him praise and honor His name because, besides Him, there is none like the true and living God who is in heaven.

### Ecclesiastes 12: 13

*Let us hear the conclusion of the whole matter: Fear God, and keep his commandments: for this is the whole duty of* man.

### Isaiah 44:8 (KJV)

[8] Fear ye not, neither be afraid: have not I told thee from that time, and have declared *it*? ye *are* even my witnesses. Is there a God beside me? yea, *there is* no God; I know not *any*.

### Genesis 2:21

God caused a deep sleep to come upon Adam, and God took out of Adam or from Adam, a rib; all that time, the rib that God took from Adam represents Eve, Adam did not know of this, but God knew because He is the One who put her there for the right time that He purposes in His will. Adam had surgery, and the doctor was the great physician; His name is Jesus.

*You and I need surgery of our hearts and mind to remove all evil thoughts and all kinds of unrighteousness that we have stored within ourselves so that our God may have that Father and children fellowship. Since our heart is where evil comes from, let us ask our God to rid us of the influence of all satanic germs. Knowing that our hearts will be pure and free of any Satanic contaminants, now let us enter the holy place where God is waiting for us to commune with us because He said, if we seek Him, we will find Him, let us all go and seek our Lord at the place where we left him knowing He is waiting for us. By reading His Holy Word, always praying, entering not into sinful acts, worshiping Him, and praising our Lord, we will find Him.*

God took a rib from man (Adam) and made a woman (Eve) from that one rib. Isn't our God great, Wonderful, and Awesome in His doings? And after the Lord God made the woman, He gave her to Adam to be his wife. It is the same thing we do now; the father gives his daughter to the man that is marrying her, for them to become one as the Lord planned it to be.

**Genesis 2:23 (KJV)**

*23 And Adam said, This is now bone of my bones, and flesh of my flesh: she shall be called Woman, because she was taken out of Man.*

After God made the woman, the Lord gave the woman to the man, and they become husband and wife, fulfilling God's plan for them and giving us examples to follow. The scripture informed us that they were no longer two separate persons; even though they both have their independent bodies; spiritually, they are one. The scripture also informed us that the man is to leave his father and mother and cleave to his wife. Furthermore, the scripture told us what God has joined together, let no man put asunder. By the scriptures, we have come to the knowledge of God's word that He is the One who establishes marriage, and He also tells us in His word how we ought to live in peace and have a successful relationship in our marriage.

Despite the corruption and the filthiness that some leaders carry out to change what God has already done, they will not succeed for long. When we as mankind interfere with God's perfect will, He will find us guilty of rebellion, and that's exactly what the serpent did to Eve in the garden of Eden. Some of us are changing God's perfect will concerning marriage to filthiness or uncleanness, all seems to be well now, but God will recompense each of them and us for what we have chosen to do to corrupt the institution of marriage.

It does not matter how much money you have; it does not represent love because so many people do not have much money, yet they are so happy than many who have so much money. When we, as human beings, have the true love of God in our hearts, we will experience peace. The ones who have less look up to God and trust Him and depend upon Him to supply their daily bread, strength, and sound mind, but many of those who are rich rely on what they already have, not knowing that they too need God in their lives.

We are not against riches, please do not get us wrong, because Abraham, Job and Solomon, and many others in the Bible were rich in wealth, but their money was not their God; instead, their God was their money because if it was not for their God, they could not have achieved what they did possess.

### Genesis 2:24 (KJV)

*²⁴ Therefore shall a man leave his father and his mother,*
*and shall cleave unto his wife: and they shall be one flesh.*

God's plan for man is that when he marries a woman and she becomes his wife; that both will build a home together in love, peace, and harmony; this is Almighty God's plan for the husband and wife. God's plan for them is that when they are ready, they will have children according to the scripture, **Genesis 1:28** and that the husband is the head of his household and his wife, taking care of them in the Lord. According to scripture, as they are blessed with children from the Lord, both parents should train them and nurture them in fear of the Lord God.

**Ephesians 5:23 (KJV)**

[23] For the husband is the head of the wife, even as Christ is the head of the church: and he is the saviour of the body.

## *Notes:*

The husband's responsibility is to have a house or an apartment to put his wife in before marriage; this is called preparation. Then, after they are married, they become husband and wife; the husband is supposed to take his wife from her parent's house to their own place or house according to the principle structure that he has already prepared to take this house and make it a home. This is how it is supposed to be; however, circumstances arise in one's life that causes things not to go the way they should. That is why the husband is to leave his parents' home and cleave to his wife, and they are to be one flesh according to the scripture, fulfilling the will of Almighty God as He already ordains it to be. And when they have children in the home that they have built together, they ought to grow the children in fear of the Lord and teach them the correct way of life.

**Proverbs 22:6 (KJV)**

[6] *Train up a child in the way he should go: and when he is old, he will not depart from it.*

## *Notes:*

When humanity does as Almighty God commanded by His commandments, we will have no problem with each other and even the devil, he will try, but you will be ready for him like King Jesus did. But when we choose to please our fleshly desires without regard for others, we become problematic and prey to the enemies. At the same time, Satan takes advantage of us through our disobedience to Almighty God and uses us to be a vessel of chaos, which in turn, we become a vessel of dishonor.

When humanity refuses to follow the Lord's instructions as He has given them to us stated in the book of commandments "The Bible" and chooses to do whatever we feel like doing whenever we feel like, we will always experience problems in our lives. At that time, we are operating in our own will, and that is called **"Self Will"** this is very dangerous to our lives because when humanity does not respect the law of Almighty God, we become a covenant breaker. Our greatest enemy, the devil, will come into our lives and amplify his wicked plan and destroy us or use us to be his destroyer towards others.

One of the husband's responsibilities is to guard his home against both physical and spiritual enemies. Husbands, we must pray and seek God for direction for our family, always praying for our wives so that the devil will not use her to cause confusion in the marriage. As the devil lied to Eve to deceive Adam, the devil has not stopped his operational plans of destruction towards us. He is continuously attacking humanity. After all, he is hateful towards us because his days are getting closer to his end, so he is rampaging like a bully, doing the same thing he did back then, using many different devices to accomplish his evil goal. His goal is to have us human beings disobey Almighty God, which is sin. Also, he wants us to fight against each other and kill one another in anger, and then we will end up in hell like him in due time. How many of us can honestly say that the devil is succeeding in his work? Look at what is happening in the world, confusion, chaos, wars, killings, hate, malice, jealousy, lies, upon lies like Satan.

Satan has us hurting and destroying one another in many ways, shapes, and fashion, and we believe it is for a good cause, but in the mind of the Lord God, it is wrong; therefore, when you have sinned, the penalty is death according to the scripture.

Husbands, Almighty God, did not give you a woman to be your darling wife so that you can mistreat her at your own will. When a husband decides to inflict hurt on his wife or any other man, you are doing Satan's bidding, and now you are like him to steal, kill, and destroy. It is wrong, not because God said that man is the head of the house, give us men the right to rule as a dictator or a slave master, we need to stop this foolish behavior now. Let us not be foolish in our ways, do the right things in Jesus Christ's holy name, so that you can please your God in heaven. Remember, the Lord God has commanded us to love one another. It is time to stop hurting each other in any way that we are doing it. Let us not be an instrument for Satan's destructive and manipulating gain. Many of us have the spirit of Jezebel; remember what she did? She takes by force and kills, threatening others to kill them, a very manipulating spirit that destroys and devours just because she could. Now, some of us have taken on these characteristics and displayed them upon innocent people. Some husbands are continually cheating on their wives with another woman; you are committing adultery, which is a sin. We know that you would not like your wife to cheat on you, then why are you doing it to her?

Many men are beating their wives as if they are fighting someone in the street. Is this the reason why you marry her? Some husband disrespects their wife in public places; this does not seem right at all. Would you mind changing your ways? Some animals are treated with more respect and love than how some men treat their wives. Yes, some wife treats their husband the same as trash. Do you see how some people treat their dogs at the park or on the street, yet they don't have love in their hearts for some people when God commands us to love one another. We have been getting the method wrong for many years now; we are no longer a child, grow up as gentlemen and women, boys and girls, obey God and His Son Jesus Christ and start to love people.

Knowing that some people treat their animals so much better than how some husbands treat their wives should never be a comparison, but it is necessary. An animal is an animal, and a human being is precious in Almighty God's sight; that is why we are made to be like Him. Is this the expectation of what Almighty God expects from you when He made the woman? I surely know it's not! Some husbands have thrown their wives out of her home and replaced them with other women. Since when have we become so foolish? Don't we fear the rebuke of God almighty? Yes, we know that sometimes some wives follow other domineering wives who are ruling their husband and family with a strong arm, but she is out of control according to the scripture, and your wife may listen to that wife and bring it home not knowing someone else home is not her own.

Husbands, before you get so quick to send your wife away from her home, please take time out and honestly examine yourself, and you will find that you are also guilty of something. So Jesus said in **St. John 8:7.** So why not have a conversation and find out what the problem is? Yes, it could be you; nevertheless, let's have a conversion.

We also know that it is impossible to live with some women in this present world; it seems as if they are possessed with the spirit of Jezebel, "the Jezebel spirit," very unruly and have no respect for her husband. Unfortunately, there are many husbands like her too. This spirit takes over at any cost destroying whoever or whatever is in the way, manipulating others in every aspect that you can think about even worse. It is very selfish, just for self and cares not much for others, such as husband, children, and home, unless they will be recognized, drawing attention to self "full of pride and rotten inside."

The husband should protect his wife from her in-laws, which is the husband's side of the family; he should not allow his side of the family to disrespect his wife during his presence or absence. His wife is to do the same, that her side of the family should not attack her husband physically or by words of disrespect. Relationships and marriage are essential and should be protected from family members, friends, relatives, or spirits so that the bond of love will survive the spiritual promises. God is the one who establishes this institution, and when two people get married, His will for them is to live in peace with each other. Remember that the wife is the husband's helpmeet; she is to help her husband in every area that her help is needed for the betterment of self and family, and he the husband must allow his wife to exercise her godly role to fulfill the will of God.

## *Children in the family that is not biological*

When a man has children in another relationship, it is the sole responsibility of that man, the father of those children, to see that they respect his wife. She is not their biological mother but is now their new mom. Yes, they are not her biological children, but he must teach and train them to have the ultimate respect for his wife, their Mom. And the wife is to love those children who are not her biological children as if they were her children so that love, peace, and harmony will be in the home. Please remember that the child or those children have no decisions concerning why their parents are no longer in love and cause them to leave the marriage or relationship for a new one.

Therefore, when a child or children follow one parent into another relationship, that man or woman must at all times know that they are not just getting involved or having a relationship with each other. That child or those children must be a part of this comprehensive new family. They did not choose this new family; you have chosen it for them. Therefore, the father and mother must ensure that they are treated with love and respect, with no exceptions.

When you eat and drink, they must be a part-taker of the meal too. When you sleep, the children must have a decent bed to sleep on too. When your biological child or children go to school, do not forget those who are not your biological child, they must also enroll in school. Remember that child or children are now yours'; if you know that you cannot accept them, you should never get involved with that man or woman. When you give your biological children the leg and breast of the chicken, do not provide your non-biological children with the chicken's back or even the feet, this is not good in the sight of God who sees your action and behavior. Mothers, some of you neglected your children for a man because of love and allowed him to treat them worse than garbage. Is this fair in the sight of God? Examine yourself, get back on track, and ask God, your Father in heaven, to help you in your sad relationship and your confused mind.

It is the wife's responsibility to see that her children who came into the marriage to live in her husband's house, they too must do the same in respecting him, giving him the respect that he deserved from them. "Women seek love, but men look for respect" When a man is respected, in his mind, he knows that you love him because he believes that if you did not love him, you would not respect him; nevertheless, not in every case. However, it does not always work out exactly how you have planned it because many people are complicated in their ways and thoughts. All this is for peace in the home; without peace, there is no happiness, and with love, there will be no hate. When these two meet each other, guess what?

## *Wives and Mom*

Wives do not give your biological child or children the best of everything, and the children that are not yours get the worst of everything because this is wickedness, and their Father in heaven sees your evil towards them, and you will not be guiltless.

In some families, the children of one parent sometimes mistreat them because they are not their flesh and blood because of the wickedness in the step-parents' hearts. The name step-parent does fit many because that's all they do, step upon those that are not their own child. So, stepping all over those children that are not yours is the godly thing to do? What if you should pass away in death? Would you like if the table turns against your children, Oh no, sow good seed and let the Lord Jesus bless your goodness and those seeds will follow you and your family?

When a parent is no more because of death, this man or woman comes into the children's home and treats them horribly without regard as if they are not human beings; this is terrible and wicked, and their Father in heaven will not hold you guiltless. We sometimes speak and pray that the Lord will watch over the motherless, but if you are the new mom and dad in their lives, you are now the mother to the motherless and the father to the fatherless.

None of the parents should allow their children to bully the other child/children, not because they are not their biological siblings. Many of us have not yet understood what love and peace are because if many of us genuinely deserve these two areas in our lives, we would make sure that we give them to others. Be very careful of what you are sowing because one day, you surely will reap that which you have sown in the time of your harvest.

Every marriage is subject to trials and temptations by the devil. God will use those trials and sorrows that you are going through as a test to see where your heart is if you will give into the devices of the enemy, or will you stand on the word of God by **Faith** and the commitment that you have made to yourself and your wife or husband.

Satan seeks to destroy everything good and bring confusion in our lives to have doubts concerning God. Every time the devil is at work, call on Jesus because He is the only One who has defeated Satan and all his agents of darkness. Jesus has already defeated him on the cross, but it is left for us to believe that Jesus indeed went to the cross and that He has nailed all your sickness, diseases, burden, confusions, demon's oppression, and so much more on the cross. Satan knows how much the Father and His Son, Jesus Christ, loved us, and he wants to come between our relationship with our Lord Jesus. It is the same on the earth, Satan wants to come between husband and wife to cause the connection to experience stress, and too much pressure will cause divorce, which is not of God. Our enemy seeks to separate us from heavenly things, and by doing so, he can cause us to forfeit eternal life. Let us stop and investigate or examine our lives, and we will see the enemy at work. Let us stop Satan and all his agents of darkness by **resisting** him; the scripture said this.

**James 4:7 (KJV)**

*7 Submit yourselves therefore to God. Resist the devil, and he will flee from you.*

**Genesis 3**

Satan was not after Eve; Adam was his target, but examine how he got to Adam. Eve was just an instrument that was available to be used by our enemy, Satan. What did he do?

**Genesis 3:1 (KJV)**

*1 Now the serpent was more subtle than any beast of the field which the LORD God had made. And he said unto the woman, Yea, hath God said, Ye shall not eat of every tree of the garden?*

According to the scripture, Satan influences the serpent; the serpent was the most subtle in the garden. After the serpent was influenced, he becomes an agent for Satan to carry out his lie, which is to deceive; that is what a lie is: deceiving someone. The serpent went to Eve, the wife of Adam, and spoke to her and changed God's word and added one word in the sentence. Eve, in turn, believes the serpent and does exactly what God said not to do. But nothing happens then or right away until Adam saw his wife, the man whom

God gave the commandments, took from his wife, Eve, the fruit and eat, for he was the head of the garden. Therefore, Satan achieved his goal, and that was to infiltrate man to get to God. But God has already had a plan for humanity's **Deliverance,** and this deliverance is by His Son Jesus Christ.

Let us put the devil to shame by resisting him so the devil will not use your children to destroy your marriage, your friends, even the rest of your extended family members. Listen to God and God alone because people will come into your life in Sheep clothing, but underneath they are wolves. Ask God for the **Spirit of discernment** so that you will be able to discern the spirits around you and their operations because the scriptures said, try the spirit by the Spirit.

Remember this, when Almighty God made Adam and Eve by His Son Jesus; they were perfect in all sense of perfection. They were in the dispensation of **Innocence.** They were perfect and Innocence of all evil thoughts and works. They did not know how to do anything wrong because they were perfect; that is how Almighty God created them and made them like Him, the Lord God, who is perfect. But Satan wanted humanity to be like him and disobey God our Father; however, the Father does not want to share us with the devil, you and I must choose, either we are for God or the devil. All humankind was supposed to be like Adam and Eve when they were first in the garden of **Eden,** perfect.

God's plan and purpose were for all of us to be perfect and to obey Him in everything, but because of sin, we do not have the desire to please God, so that is why Jesus came to die for our sinful ways. Jesus came and purchased our freedom from Satan's prison by shedding His blood to forgive our sins, and He died for us so that we will not die spiritually, which is the second death. Unfortunately, many of us refuse to acknowledge Jesus Christ as the Son of God for who He is and His purpose for coming into the world to rescue humanity from everlasting punishment in hell.

***"There are millions upon millions of people born once and died twice, and it will continue until they accept Christ Jesus. Also, there are millions upon millions born twice and die once because they have accepted Jesus Christ as their Lord and Savior and King."***

We pray that as you read this book, the Spirit of God will convict your soul as the Father draws you by His Spirit to His Son Jesus Christ. Whenever we choose to do wrong, we follow Satan's works and take on his character, not God and His Son, Christ Jesus. Should we continue to sin against our God? The answer is no; let not sin have dominion over you, according to the scripture.

**Romans 6: 14**

*[14] For sin shall not have dominion over you: for ye are not under the law, but under grace.*

Husbands and wives, the marriage vows you have made to each other, please do not take them lightly; those words are powerful words that both of you have uttered from your mouth. It was not just to each other, but rather, both of you have also made these vows before Almighty God in heaven. God is the One who establishes marriage, and when we join in marriage, we fulfill the will of God on the earth. The Lord has ordained it in heaven, and no human beings have the authority to nullify or amend the divine constitution law of marriage. Therefore, when we break the vows, we also come against the will of God through marriage. Marriage is a serious decision; therefore, make sure that you are ready for marriage, emotionally, financially, spiritually, and physically before getting into it. Do not get into it by yourself; include Jesus in your choices.

## Side notes:

The very first thing that involves marriage is a relationship of **love,** love, and not lust. If you are not careful, you can get them wrong because it is a thin line between love and lust. Without true love, the connection of the relationship is just superficial, with no positive conduit. For example, **1st Timothy 6:10 says that *"money is the root of all evil"***. Would you please get a bible and finish reading the rest of the verse? What happens if the money fountain dries up? What happens when there is not enough money to spend? Will you still love that person? Many people go for looks rather than love; what happens if that person should have an unseen accident or illness that interferes with their appearance, that causes them not to look attracted as before? What happens then? Will you continue to love, the love of your life, as you have said?

Many love because of convenience or needs. For example, someone may not have a place to stay, and through the kindness of your kind-heartedness, you have given that person who is in need of accommodation; thanks be to the Lord God for your kind heart. Yes, you have met their needs, and now they are satisfied with a roof over their head. After a while, they rise from where they were to become fruitful in their life, praise the Lord. Sometimes a relationship materializes, and this person one day gets that big job they have applied for, and they forget you who were there for them when they were down.

Then that person moved out with little notice, some no notice at all, these are the ungrateful people that sometimes come into our lives, and we are not saying that we should not help, but we need to consult the Lord before we do everything that can or may affect us. To all those people who are in the position to help others, do it in the name of the Lord Jesus Christ so that when they hurt you, you will not be disappointed after they turn their back on you.

When that person whom you help becomes independent because doors of opportunity have arrived. After they begin to progress and make their lives worthwhile, the relationship built out of convenience is no longer valuable. That person abandoned you, the one you were there for in the time of their need, now they become successful, and you are now useless to them. These things sometimes happen in people's lives, according to these words from my wife. ***"Everyone wants to use you, but no one wants to be used by you."*** Pride of the heart, selfishness, and being ungrateful, the person who was in need no longer want to have anything to do with you the helper, and turned their back on the helper, forgetting where they were and could have been if God did not allow that kind-hearted person/s who you are to bless them.

Please do not worry about some people and their attitude or unkindness; keep on doing good because the good you do for others will follow you, your kindness should not have any strings attached to it. The Lord God and His Son Jesus Christ expected all of us to be good to one another.

Sometimes life in this present world can throw some things in our lives; it makes us wonder what happens to people. But this is who we are, many do not have God's love within themselves, and there will always be selfishness and disrespect without love. So, again, how can we give what we do not have? First, we need to know what love is and what to do with it for anyone to show love. Second, it must be cultivated and nurtured and shared among the living. No longer can the dead know that you love them, so do not go and shed your tears as if you did care for the living. Now is the time while there is life to shower love upon the ones you love. Let them experience love from you while they are alive. Do we know what love is? Do we ever share or experience true love from the dept of the heart? Doesn't it make you feel so, so good on the inside?

Therefore, if you do not have God's love inside you, you will not be able to give what you do not possess. You cannot give someone a dollar if you only have a quarter. Therefore, to have a great relationship with someone else, you need to develop love. When we were a baby or a child, we have pure love because a baby does not know what is evil, that child does not know the difference of people's skin color or where they come from, but while we are growing up, something went wrong, and these something's are what we believed happened.

According to the scriptures, it is the parents' responsibility to teach their children the fear of God and love Him first, self and others. That is the right thing to do, to love people and their neighbors as they love themselves. Teach them at a young age and let them grow up with it in their mind and heart how necessary it is to love one another. Then, because God loves them so much that He was willing to give His Son for them, the child or children, in turn, they must also love every human being, not some, but all and yes, even your enemies, according to the scriptures.

When love is not being taught in the home, the child will have to learn what they hear outside, whether good or bad, and we will be judged by the Lord of the good or bad that we do here on earth. When hate is spoken in the home, and the children hear it, they will also learn to hate; why? Because the parents do have a significant influence on their children's lives, you are the ones that they are listening to at home; therefore, be careful about what you are teaching them. You are the ones that they wake up seeing every day of their lives until they are grown up and no longer living at home or able to make their own decisions. Parents, what did you teach your children before they leave home for college? Some colleges these days are a mess, that's what I heard, is that true? We must also teach our children how to be strong for themselves to survive in this wicked and dreadful world. Many people in the world are speaking too many negative words that have been planted in the hearts of others, and they took it up and began to sow them in people's life. Some of those words have destroyed lives in the world and produced haters for others based upon where they come from or their skin color, and God will not hold anyone of you guiltless.

Marriage is not just until babies are born, but long after, marriage is for life, ***"until death do you part"*** husbands and wives, marriage is for a lifetime with each other, consider it a career. Marriage is not just a mere contract, as many think it is because they sign a marriage certificate and put a ring on their finger, but rather, it is so significant than you believe. When anyone thinks about marriage, we must also think about Almighty God because if it were not for Him, there wouldn't be a word named marriage. Everything is because of the **Lord JESUS,** and without Jesus, nothing that exists could have been according to the scripture, and we believe the scriptures.

### Revelation 4:11 (KJV)

*[11] Thou art worthy, O Lord, to receive glory and honour and power: for thou hast created all things, and for thy pleasure they are and were created.*

### John 1:3 (KJV)

*[3] All things were made by him; and without him was not any thing made that was made.*

## *Marriage and the Expectations of a Wife*

### Ephesians 5:22 (KJV)

22 Wives, submit yourselves unto your own husbands, as unto the Lord.

Wives, submit yourselves unto your own husbands according to the scriptures. The word submit is not a mere word that should be taken carelessly; it is a very profound word because it lays out the solid foundation of one of the principal roles of a wife's life towards her husband at all times or until death do they part.

**Submit:** Yield, give/ offer.

Therefore a wife is to give herself to her husband. You, the wife, must be ready to give yourself to her husband and ready to offer him yourself. And please remember, husband, this does not mean that you are to treat her any way you like; she must always be treated in a godly manner. She is to yield herself unto her husband. Many women do not like this verse in the scripture because they are rebellious to God's authority. These wives are not rebelling to their husbands only, but rather to God Himself. The scripture is not from man; neither is it of mankind, but God's word is from God. As soon as the love of God enters their hearts, then they will be able to learn how to humble themselves to God and their husband.

Let us sum up the whole matter a quote from **Proverbs**; these wives need to cultivate the fruit of the Spirit. Whenever a wife harvests the fruit of the Spirit, Oh, what a virtuous wife and a victorious woman she will be. No longer will she lives according to her self-will but in obedience to God's will.

Again, men did not write the scriptures or give this instruction, but it was and still is God. According to the scriptures, when the wife follows God's instruction, she will be blessed by the Lord through her obedience. Let us clear up something that some ignorant people are going around talking about without knowledge or understanding. Yes, it was men like us, flesh and blood, who penned the words of God to paper, no doubt about it. However, through the Holy Spirit, the Lord God and His Son Jesus Christ inspired men of old to write the words we now call the Holy Bible. Therefore, the Holy Bible is God's word for the human race to abide by; it is a map showing us the journey to heaven where God the Father dwells. And during this journey, there will be potholes, traps, valleys and all sought of things laid in the way by Satan. There will be hills to climb and valleys below during this journey, but Jesus Christ will be right there with us. Good times and rough times to enjoy and overcome. But in all of the above and more, we cannot successfully make the trip without a personal guide, and this guide name is Jesus Christ, and the Holy Spirit was sent to strengthen us and see all of us to the end. Therefore, let us obey God and not the foolishness of men.

According to the scripture, as the wife submits herself to her own husband during her obedience, she aligns herself with the plan and purposes that God has already put in place for her marriage, and the Lord will bless her through her obedience. Will there be trials? Oh yes, but her God will see her through all of them. Why? Because of obedience!

When we pray and pronounce this prayer, ***"Thy will be done on earth as in heaven,"*** when we follow and do God's commandments by following his instruction, we are fulfilling the will of Almighty God on earth. The Lord, our God, has already put in place everything that we would need in this world for our benefit to have a good life, giving Him all the praise and glory. As it is done in heaven, so shall it be done on earth because you and I have chosen to do His will. But when we rebel against His commandments, His will cannot be done on earth as in heaven.

When we rebel or resist against the commandments of the LORD God, we open the door for Satan to come into our lives and home, and when he gets there, he will have no mercy on us because he comes to steal, kill and destroy. Satan brings diseases, sicknesses, confusion, chaos, he comes to kill and destroy our lives, yet many of us refuse to believe the truth about him, the devil who is the father of all lies.

The wife must be very mindful and conscious or sober of what she is allowing into your home. The woman is a homemaker; do you see to it that your home is in good order? What is your standard for your home? Do you have your doors open for everyone to walk in and out as if your home is a shopping mall with revolving doors?

Speak to your husband in love and respect and inform him not to entertain his friends in your house or our home every week. Yes, we know that some men like to throw words in their wife's face by letting them know that it is not their home, but rather it is my home some men will say, and many like to use these words, **"I am the head of the house"** and many of us men do not know the true meaning of what those words mean according to the scripture. So there we go again, men or husbands, we are wrong; the house you have provided for you and your wife and or family is not yours; it belongs to both of you, and she makes a home in the house. Men are the provider of the home, and the wife is the keeper and homemaker of it. ***"This is the writer's thought, the husband is the CEO of their house, and the wife is the supervisor of her home."***

The husband, who is the provider, should turn the house over to his wife, and the wife, in turn, makes a home within the house. "Husband is the head of the home, and the wife is the supervisor of her home." Because of old traditions and customs, we have gone so far out of the way; some of us, very far out of the correct way, God has set things up for our prosperity. It is full-time that we ask the Lord to intervene on our behalf and change some things for us to move from that stagnant environment and the way we think. It is time for many of us to reconsider some of our habits and traditions that keep us in the same place years after years and cannot move ahead. There is no progress because of traditions and customs. Yes, some things must not change, and one of them is the gospel of the Lord Jesus Christ.

Wives, to submit yourself to your husband is not just to show him respect, which is expected of you as the wife. Respect his decisions, honor him as a man and not as God, and do not compare him to other men or someone else husband. Also, please do not put him down, meaning belittle him before the children and friends. Why are you complaining now when you use your mouth and curse him that he will come to nothing? Didn't you decree that he will be nothing? What you have spoken is what you get. So tame your tongue, and be respectful in Jesus's name. Be careful of the advice that you are receiving from others and submit yourself to him with the knowledge of God's word. Obey his decisions if it will not cause you to sin against God and to harm others. Your husband is to rule over you with respect and love, even as Christ Jesus rules over us who is the head of the man. And He is also the head of the church (spiritual church), but He does this not in wickedness, but in love, so should the husband to his wife.

Therefore, if you, the husband, expect your wife to obey you because you are the head of the house, so are you to follow Jesus Christ's instruction because He is your head. So, husband, first, you obey God to expect that obedience from your wife; let us not be a hypocrite.

Some husbands think they are now licensed to do whatever they choose to do to their wives because they are the head. You are not a slave master to your wife; she is your wife, your helpmeet "suitable for you" she is not just a baby maker, a sex machine to satisfy your sexual greed; many of us men need to have self-control. She is your helpmeet, your wife. She is somebody's child, just like you are. She is to be treated with love and respect; she is unique; that's why the Lord Jesus made her like that for you.

I have heard that many Christian men abuse their wives, beat them, hit them with their hands, and so much more. Are you not an instrument of Satan, and are you not a shame of yourself? Jesus teaches us to love and not to hate. The only hate that we Christians must possess is to hate sin. Therefore, we as Christians should not hate anyone; this is of Satan and not Jesus Christ. When someone hates another person for any reason, we hate God's creation. Why? Because God created all human beings for Himself, we are all formed in His image and after His likeness. Therefore, when we hate another human being, we hate God's creation that He made for Himself, and we are telling God that we hate what He has made.

Love is an action word; just speaking the word love does not mean much without action. Just as faith without works is dead, love without work is also dead.

Let us explain! Telling a person you love them is just words; there is no proof that you indeed do, but when you go out of your way or make some sacrifice by doing something worthwhile, caring for someone when sick. Be present when that person needs you, or even when you can cancel some appointments that may not be as important to accompany them to the doctor. Purchase something for that person without complaining about the cost and just being there when you are needed. Treating your wife like a queen supposes to be treated. Cook for her, make her a cup of hot tea if it is her likeness, and so much more that will prove that you genuinely love her. Please remember that things alone do not demonstrate love, things are vanity, but it is how you treat her with love flowing out from your heart like a fountain of water.

Loving your wife is to get a job and provide accommodation for her and the family. You should be in the position to supply food and drinks for her and the family. She and the children need clothing so that they will not be naked. Pay the bills when they are due, and so much more. I will not be naïve; many homes need the wife to step up and help financially because your husband's paycheck is just not enough to do all that is required to sustain the family. Therefore, she becomes his helpmeet in helping so that the family will live in peace and experience the blessings of the Lord. Money, money is a big problem in relationships; I pray it will not be in yours. Lack of money in some homes causes much stress, quarrels, relationships break up, and breakdown; such things should not be so. Why did you get married for money and material things or love?

Please, let us save our relationships and marriages, do not allow lack of money to cause you to destroy or throw away all those many years of good memories that each other has shared, and please do not forget the innocent children.

Be careful, ladies, because some men are very good at what they do, putting on an outstanding performance, they are like actors without a paycheck to get you into bed, and when they do, some of them change on you like bleach on colored clothing. He is no longer that persisting person pursuing you for love, supposedly; he has accomplished his agenda, just like Satan trick us with lovely things, and then he destroys our lives. We are not implying that this behavior is of all men, but many. The characteristic of their behavior is to deceive you by lying. Many men behave in such a manner to have their way with as many ladies as possible, then some of them go and broadcast it; that is what Satan does. This behavior is not and will never be of God. God in heaven is righteous, and He is holy, and He does not dwell in sin.

A better example, our Father in heaven said that he loves us, but he did not just say it; instead, He proves it to us with the ultimate sacrifice of His Son, the Lamb of God, the Lord Jesus Christ. He purchases us from slavery, and the slave master is Satan. He did not use money because the rich would afford it, and the poor would suffer and die, thank God for Jesus who gave His life for the human race. The only thing that is equal in this world is salvation. Why? It came to us the same way from one God, our Father in heaven. Jesus Christ dies on the same cross for all human beings. Jesus gave all human beings the same gift, the gift of life through His death on the cross. The same blood for our forgiveness.

Jesus died so that all, in turn, receive Eternal life through the shedding of His blood. Jesus purchases us by shedding His precious blood and dying for us. Thus, God the Father proves His love for us by His Son Jesus Christ, and Jesus proves His love for all of us by shedding His blood and dying on the cross. Again, the only thing in this world that is equal and is given equally is salvation, and every promise of equality from men is a lie.

### John 15:12-14 (KJV)

*[12] This is my commandment, That ye love one another, as I have loved you.*

*$^{13}$ Greater love hath no man than this, that a man lay down his life for his friends.*

*$^{14}$ Ye are my friends, if ye do whatsoever I command you.*

According to the scripture, husbands, your wife is the weaker vessel; therefore, we must treat them tenderly, knowing what the scripture said. Some women out there are strong, some are stronger than some men physically, but that's not a complete interpretation of what the meaning truly is; it is not just about physical strength. The Bible says that they are the weaker vessel; no matter how physically strong they are, God said they are the weaker vessel, and that's what they are. Emotionally most of them are soft, weak only in some instances because that's how God makes them; the structure of the male muscle mass is not the same as a woman. Women are very tenderhearted, so they are more emotionally connected to the ones they love dearly. When a woman love, she gives her whole heart, mind, and life; she is easily connected to, more than a man.

**1 Peter 3:7 (KJV)**

*$^{7}$ Likewise, ye husbands, dwell with them according to knowledge, giving honour unto the wife, as unto the weaker vessel, and as being heirs together of the grace of life; that your prayers be not hindered.*

Husbands, consider a rose garden, "yes, many women love roses," but let us stop here. Let us visit the flower shop or wherever roses are sold. That beautiful bunch of roses did not just happen like that; the gardener cultivates these roses spent valuable time preparing the ground to plant those rose plants. He has to nourish them by adding plant food and other things needed for the plants' success. They need water and sunlight for better yield. He takes time to remove anything that would cause the rose plant not to grow correctly, and he pulls up weeds that would cause his garden of roses not to flourish so that they will be ready for the flower shop or store. The consumers will be buying roses for their loved ones, and it should not be done only because of special events, but now and then, surprise her with a beautiful bunch of roses or plants.

It is the same thing with our wives; she is like a rose in a garden "wasn't Eve in the garden of Eden?" We must cultivate love; we must take care so that nothing pollutes our love for our wives or husbands. We must work to maintain love in our relationship. We must nurture our relationship. We must see that no unkind friends, demons, physical or spiritual enemies come into your garden (your home) to spoil your wife and destroy your marriage.

Satan did that to Eve. Adam was supposed to protect his wife Eve from outside influences, but he failed, many may not agree, but it's ok. Unfortunately, some of us are doing just what happens in the garden of Eden; we are not protecting the home from Satanic invasion; as soon as something goes wrong in our marriage, we threaten each other with divorce. Did God tell anyone of us to do so? Oh yes, He did, but under what circumstances did Jesus say that we could? Also, did He say that we can remarry after a divorce?

And if we think yes, let us consider what Jesus said about the law. Let us consider within our self, have we done enough to save our marriage? Maybe there is another alternate reason why some of us are so quick to divorce; what could that be? Perhaps another woman is waiting to see another woman home destroyed or break up so that she can come in and take over. Miss, do you know that he is married? Would you like someone to go into your home, destroy it, and cause your marriage to dissolve? Please reconsider what you are allowing this man to get you into, what we sow, surely one day we shall reap. When reaping time comes, will you be able to stand?

## *Explanation:*

*The gardener is the husband, and the garden is the home you and your wife (spouse) have built together. The roses are your wife; first, the children also share this garden. Second, it is the husband's responsibility to make a good foundation of love within the home. His wife is to be nourished with love, respect, care for, emotional support, and give her attention, even though some spouse needs much more attention, because she may go out and look for attention outside and violate the principle of the marital relationship. If this should happen, she invites Satan into her home and trusts God's word; the family lives will never be the same.*

The husband's responsibility is to teach his wife about the love of God, and they both teach the children. The children are part of the family tree; therefore, they are a part of this garden. Children in a home become collateral damage when domestic or foreign danger threatens the family and Satan's devices, and he is a deadly enemy.

When a couple is in the process of getting a divorce or get a divorce, the husband or the wife is not the only one who is experiencing hurt, shame, and disgrace. But many couples do not care or realize the children's emotional pain, psychological hurts, and vulnerability to turn to deadly substances as their comfort. Some of us are all about pleasing ourselves to get what we want without considering others. Husbands, let us drive the enemies out of our home and ask the Lord Jesus to destroy the enemies' works in your marriage. Ask Him to render them powerless. Husbands pray for your wife every day, and wives, pray for your husband every day, and both must pray for the children every day, knowing that the enemies can use them to get into your home to devour and destroy.

Let your garden bloom with lots of love pebbles; water the garden with much love, giving way to peace with yourself and the household. Be always sober and vigilant with the things around you so that the family will be aware of their surroundings. Satan, the enemy, hates what God has joined together, and since he is a destroyer, he will do anything to destroy your relationship and marriage, even your life. The remedy is the word of God and prayer with Jesus Christ as your center post.

## *Husbands*

### *Ephesians 5:28 (KJV)*

### *Notes:*

*A husband ought to love his wife like unto his own body. According to the scripture, if a husband does not love his wife, he does not love his own body, for he that hateth his wife hateth himself. No man that loveth himself will at any time hurt himself, but if he hateth himself, he will hurt anyone at any time.*

*According to the scripture, when a husband or a single man hurts his wife or girlfriend that he professes to love, you become a liar to yourself because you and your wife are one. According to the true meaning of love, no male should inflict pain or verbal abuse upon the one they love. After you have a quarrel or conflict with yourself, how do you feel? There will be some misunderstanding in a relationship, but they don't have to be a war.*

### **Ephesians 5:31 (KJV)**

*31 For this cause shall a man leave his father and mother, and shall be joined unto his wife, and they two shall be one flesh.*

### *Notes:*

When two people get married, they are no longer two separate persons, even though they are physically, but spiritually the Lord Jesus said they are one. One in unity, one in love, one in agreement, one in decision-making, and so much more. The Lord wants us to be like the God-head, Father, Son, and Holy Spirit; they are three separate persons, but they are one in every aspect of Oneness in Unity.

> Husbands should not have a separate bedrooms and the wives the same, exceptions, only for some isolation because of sickness or illness that may cause that temporary separation, God knows. When a couple is angry with each other, each person should come together and solve the issue whatever it may be before going to bed (sleep) according to the scripture, **Ephesians 4:26**

> Husbands should not be hiding their money in a separate Bank Account. Where is the love? Remember oneness? Remember, Husbands, the Lord Jesus commands us through the word of God to love our wives as we love our self.

Husbands, just some of us, would you cheat on yourself? If you love your wife as you love yourself, you would not? If not, why are you cheating on your wife? And wife, why are you cheating on your husband? An extramarital relationship is disrespectful to the innocent spouse, and many do it without regard for the other person's feelings. I know that the husband and single men would not want the same to happen to them, so why are you treating her, your wife, or your girlfriend with such disrespect? And if pregnancy should result in the affair, then to hide sin, abortion is recommended. Through our own carelessness, many times, we hurt ourselves.

Every husband is commanded to love their wife as Christ Jesus loved us and gave His life for us the spiritual church. Only those saved by the blood of Jesus are called the church, the spiritual church that Jesus Christ is returning to receive unto Himself. Nevertheless, He shed His blood for all humanity. However, not all will come to accept Jesus Christ as their Lord and Savior so that they, too, will become a part of the spiritual church. If you are not saved meaning, surrender your life to Jesus and let Him wash and cleanse you from your sins so that you will become a child of God just like many before you. What are you waiting for? Surrender your life to Jesus Christ right now? Many of us are missing something or someone most important in our lives, and that someone is Jesus Christ. Without Him, we are nothing; let us seek Him so that He can be the head of our lives. **ST. John 15:5**

Many wives behave like some men, walking up and down in the earth looking and seeking men to sleep with, even though they have their husbands at home or perhaps it's her profession. Your behavior is like a foolish woman who builds her home and then digs it down to the ground with your mouth in one day. Again, your behavior is selfish, disrespectful to your marital vows, sinning against God and yourself. Yes, you are breaking the commandment. Thou shalt not commit adultery. Many women are out there in the street selling their bodies for money, thus saith the Lord, your body is the temple of the Holy Ghost, stop this behavior right now and repent and receive forgiveness. But if you don't need the Holy Ghost to dwell within you, then something else will come and take up residence in you instead of the Holy Spirit, and that something will drag you into the pit of hell.

**Exodus 20:14 (KJV)**

*[14] Thou shalt not commit adultery.*

It is time, gentlemen, and ladies, throughout the earth, we need to obey the Lord your God if you believe that God in heaven is the only true God, and He is the One who created you and made you. Created you, yes, your spirit and soul were created by God the Father, by His Son Jesus Christ, and your body was made from the dust of the ground by Creator God. Worship Him who created you and not any other things or people who cannot forgive you of your sins and cannot give you eternal life. No human being has everlasting life in themself to give to another; only Jesus Christ has this life in Him by His Father who art in heaven. The Father gave His Son this life to provide us with, but we must turn from sin to righteousness.

## *To husbands and all men*

It has been reported on Television, Radio, the Internet, and whatever other media; some women have experienced horrible treatment at the hands of their husbands or male friends. Many have been killed or seriously injured, mental and psychological trauma from the hands of wickedness and evil, which is of the devil, and it ought not to be so. Husbands, your wife is the bone of your bone, and she is the flesh of your flesh to those who are married. So why are you hurting your own flesh? What has happened? Have you allowed Satan to enter your heart and cause you to be violent to your spouse or friends to carry out such a wicked act on your wife or girlfriend/fiancé?

What could she have ever done to you that would cause you to kill (murder) yourself, that is your wife? We have done worse to the Lord God, and yet He has not gone around killing us for our wrongs, yet He is patiently waiting for us to come to Him and ask Him to forgive us of all our faults. But we must thank the Lord Jesus for His precious blood that was shed for our forgiveness. God the Lord extended His **Mercies** towards us, and **Forgiveness** is available by God our Father because if it were not for the blood of the Lord Jesus Christ that brought forgiveness, we all would be consumed by the wrath of the Father. The Lord did not destroy us for our wrongs, but we are ready to hurt or kill others as soon as they offend us. Why?

Please remember that she is now joined together with you as one flesh according to the scripture from God. What has she done? Why would you raise your hand and make a fist to strike her, and many have done it? Aren't you hurting your flesh? What could she have done that would allow you to bring another woman into her matrimonial home, and many of us men take her unto your wife's marital bed and insult your wife into her bedroom? The scripture said that we should not defile the marriage bed.

**Hebrews 13:4 (KJV)**

> [4] *Marriage is honourable in all, and the bed undefiled:*
> *but whoremongers and adulterers God will judge.*

What did she do? Why did you choose to insult her in front of your friends? Would you like her to do the same as you have done her? I know that you would not like it because her life may be in danger when you get home, not all men, but many abusers.

Your hands that Jesus gave you are to lift them to God your Father in worship and praise to Him, also, a form of surrendering to Him. It is to caress your wife. Your hands are to be used to work and support your wife and the children, your family, and no other woman should be a part-taker of your family money, time, except for benevolence. If there are children from another relationship, of course, they need your time and money too as their father.

Husbands, your wife should never discourage you at any time, not to support your child or children that are not living with you. If this should happen, it is an evil suggestion, and whoever insists that it should not happen is selfishness of your heart. The children need to eat and drink too. They need clothe on their body and a roof over their head. They need school materials, and they also need your time with them. So much more can be said about the excellent use of men's hands, helping the homeless, those in need, and more, but never to use them to hurt any female at any time. Ladies, this includes all females, do not provoke the man to anger.

I heard that some women have a very mean spirit, "bad ladies," please stop it, it is not comely of you to behave in such a manner. Oh yes, in this wicked and sinful world, I know it is tough for some of you ladies to get ahead; it is also challenging for those who live in countries with no regard for women. Many men have used customs and traditions to keep their wives and young ladies in a **psychological** prison. Men, this too is one of the areas that Jesus came to deliver you from, turn from your old traditions and customs that are not relevant these days because it bears no fruit, and it causes the word of God to be of none effect. See below,

**Matthew 15:3 (KJV)**

*[3] But he answered and said unto them, Why do ye also transgress the commandment of God by your tradition?*

**Matthew 15:6 (KJV)**

*[6] And honour not his father or his mother, he shall be free. Thus have ye made the commandment of God of none effect by your tradition.*

Please remember that the woman you marry is somebody's child; when you hurt her physically or even cause her to be demise, the parents of that child, their daughter, who is your wife, is also hurting. It may not mean anything to you, but it is their child that you, her husband, or boyfriend just killed, "murdered," or seriously injured. Why? There are few, could be many, that the wife has done the same. Wives or girlfriends, why? What could have caused you to do such? The word of God said this,

**Ephesians 4:26-27 (KJV)**

*[26] Be ye angry, and sin not: let not the sun go down upon your wrath:*

*[27] Neither give place to the devil.*

When we do not have God's love within our hearts, we can do evil. The absence of love is hate, and the lack of prayer is evil thoughts, not in all cases, but many. So we need to get back to the basics, having God in our lives and home again. When God is absent from our house, evil spirits will come and take up residence and fill that void. When Jesus is the center of your marriage, relationship, and in your children, and everything and everywhere, the devil will try, but he will not be successful. When you are anchored on the Rock of all ages, who is Jesus Christ, the devil cannot penetrate your lives and home. If he should, either you have left a door open for him to enter in, or the Lord allowed him for a purpose, like Job in the Bible, he was being tested by the Lord, and you and I are no different. When this happens, we need to find out from God if we are the one who is responsible for what is happening, or if this is God's doing, testing you, then you will know what to do, again we say like Job in the Bible.

When a woman or wife is working, and your salary is much greater than your husband's, please do not use it and put him down or belittle him to make him feel as if he is less than a man. Thank God that you have a good-paying job, but it does not give you a license to use this blessing to curse him or put him down. Some wives have a much better paying job than their husbands, which does not mean that you, the wife, have become the head of the household. If you think so, you are out of the will of Almighty God.

When two people are married, no longer should each other's money belongs to self, but the money that comes into the household belongs to you as a family, or the one that is more mature to manage money. It is to pay the bills, groceries, college funds, savings, and such forth. According to the scripture, let us not be selfish; both of you are now husband and wife, one flesh. Therefore, conduct yourself with honor and respect for each other so that your God will be well pleased with each of you. Neither should anyone in the marriage have their secret bank account or unless you genuinely do not love each other. Also, men, don't be a lazy person and allow your wife to be the only one that is financially supporting the household other than if you are sick and cannot work again.

The wife should not have any problem if her husband needs to take care of his parents by spending money on them, or even so, the husband should not have any problem if his wife needs to help her parents. When the relationship is lovely with good open communication, no one of the spouses will sneak and go behind the other and do things without knowing it. We cannot continue to live our lives in hate, selfishness, lies, and ignorance. Let us not give place to the devil to take advantage of us through the opportunity that we have allowed him to get against us and be successful. Let us resist him, and he will flee according to the scripture.

**James 4:7**

From now on, allow love to flourish in your relationship like a beautiful bunch of roses towards your spouse. So watered the relationship, do not let love die for any reason at all. Whenever you have done wrong to your spouse, you should apologize to each other and move on, don't think you should not apologize to your wife and children when you are wrong because you are a man. Very important in a relationship and marriage. Learn to forgive, have a forgiven heart, please move on, do not get stuck in your past mistakes, rebuild on the foundation that has already existed, and live in peace in Jesus Christ's precious name.

***Amen.***

# CHAPTER FIVE

## *What is True Love*

**1 Corinthians 13:4-5 (KJV)**

*[4] Charity suffereth long, and is kind; charity envieth not; charity vaunteth not itself, is not puffed up,*

*[5] Doth not behave itself unseemly, seeketh not her own, is not easily provoked, thinketh no evil;*

In a relationship and marriage, each person must be committed to the relationship and marriage. When a couple makes a promise to each other, please try and keep it, and if something happens, that causes anyone not to carry out the commitment, talk about it and explain why so that none of you will blame the other. Also, each person must be faithful to the other in the relationship and marriage. Finally, each person must have a forgiving spirit within them to be a forgiven person. In relationships and marriage, mistakes sometimes happen, and these mistakes need to be addressed and understood, and the errors need to be handled carefully with wisdom and forgiveness. Some of us are selfish and refuse to forgive the one who offended us, but they quickly want you who offended them to understand their mistake and forgive when they made their error. Therefore, please remember that you need to have these qualities in your marriage.

Be committed_______________________________________________

Been faithful________________________________________________

Be forgiven_________________________________________________

## The word *Charity* means **Love**

Love is the foundation of our existence as human beings or humankind. It was and still is love why God created us in His image and made us after His likeness. It is love why God, our heavenly Father, sent His Only-begotten Son Jesus Christ into this wicked and sinful world to die for all humanity's sins. If the Lord God should come right now, we believe that the church is not fully ready to receive Jesus Christ their Lord. But the Holy Father is giving us time to repent; however, He is very close at His coming; let us be ready brethren, friends, and neighbors. If the Lord should come now, we believe millions upon millions of souls will be lost for eternity. Seek the face of the Lord and turn from your wicked ways and Jesus will forgive you, and you and millions will live and not die in their sins. The dispensations of this present world or life that we are living will one day end. The evil on this earth, the hate for one another, the power struggle, and wanting more power is never-ending will one day end. So why shouldn't the Lord come now and destroy Satan's works, the Devil, including our wickedness to each other? Because He loves each one of us so much that He does not mind waiting, "Patience or Longsuffering," but there is coming a time when the Lord God shall no longer tolerate our wickedness. If God should end the world as it is right now, more likely ninety-seven percent of humanity will go to hell, but because of His love for us, and it is not His will for anyone to perish. Therefore, He the Father is giving all of us time to repent of our sins and accept His only begotten Son, Jesus Christ.

But there is coming a day which no man knows of when God shall send His Son Jesus Christ to go and receive or take away His children, the righteous people, out of this wicked and sinful world.

And these are the ones who are washed with the precious blood of Jesus, separated for Himself. Because of love, the Father will give all those who were not saved before the rapture another chance to accept His only begotten Son, Jesus Christ, and even after the period of severe troubles in the world, many will still have time to be saved. However, during that time, life on earth will not be easy.

Nevertheless, it will be God's word coming to pass, meaning that which He has spoken is now manifested, being fulfilled because He knows human beings' hearts that many will not repent according to the Bible. The only difference is the trial and tribulation that people will experience to make it right with God the Father and His Son Jesus Christ. Let no one fool you; love is the **principal** thing with God, not forgetting **obedience** is the most important, because if you obey the Lord, we will love, and that's why He commanded us to love one another as He has loved us. One more breaking news before we go further, please don't believe anyone when they give a time and date when Jesus Christ will be coming back, do not for one moment believe their report; they are all liars.

The Father said this in His word,

**1 Thessalonians 5:1-2 (KJV)**

1 But of the times and the seasons, brethren, ye have no need that I write unto you.

2 For yourselves know perfectly that the day of the Lord so cometh as a thief in the night.

**Matthew 22:36-40 (KJV)**

*36 Master, which is the great commandment in the law?*

*37 Jesus said unto him, Thou shalt love the Lord thy God with all thy heart, and with all thy soul, and with all thy mind.*

*38 This is the first and great commandment.*

*39 And the second is like unto it, Thou shalt love thy neighbour as thyself.*

*40 On these two commandments hang all the law and the prophets.*

Every human being ought to love God, the Father who created and made all of us first; our first love belongs to the Lord. Next, you must also love yourself as you are; God is the One who made you, and no one else, therefore, love you for you. Then you must love others who is your neighbor as the Lord has commanded you; according to the scripture, the Lord commanded us to love Him the LORD with all of our heart, soul, mind. **Deuteronomy 6:5** also stated that we should love the Lord with all of our might or strength. Above, we did not include your spouse because your love for your spouse is actually you? Remember, One flesh.

The Lord God is not forcing anyone to love Him, It is either you love Him, the Lord, or Satan, the Devil. The same thing that the Father expects from the husband and wife is that they will love each other so that His love will be in their lives and others will see God's love shining fort through them.

**"Love can never be money, and money can never be love."** Money is essential in our lives, but for no reason should any sensible person distorts the true meaning of love by loving someone because they have money. Below is the characteristic of the manifestation of love according to the scriptures. Please consider the value of love; true love comes from the heart and not from the mind. Love must come from the heart first, and then it is manifested within the mind.

**"Also, love is not sex, and sex cannot be and never will be love."** The true meaning of love should allow the manifestation of sex to come forth, but humanity has distorted the true meaning of love and sex, and many changes sex for love. Many people may say that when someone is not in the mode for sexual intercourse, they don't love them, and if they did love them, they would not deny them pleasure. Sex should be the benefit of love and not the main reason for love.

**Question:** What if there is an illness or surgery that may cause your spouse not to be able to satisfy your sexual needs or greed for a while? Does that account for lack of love? Of course not! Some situations arise in many people's lives that would deny them sexual pleasure with their spouse, and if there is no real love for that person, the other will go and cheat. Love keeps and causes an actual bond.

Can you imagine someone mixing concrete with sand alone? It will not hold, but if you add cement to it, there is a bonding agent in the cement that attaches itself to the sand and creates a bond, becoming a force of strength. It is the same with relationships and marriages; without genuine love for each other, the slightest turbulence, the marriage is broken into pieces. We should not love our girlfriend because we can have sex with her, if that is it, you genuinely do not love her, and the same goes for spouses and other ladies. Without love, you are just a living, empty soul waiting. What? Haven't you understood that it is the love of God why He created you and made you in His image and after His likeness? God is love, and He loves you. God needs us human beings to do the very same, love one another with the love that He gave you while you were in your mother's womb. But since you grew up and can make your own decisions, you have allowed Satan to enter your mind and sow hate within your heart, and now you are spewing out deadly poison like a serpent, ready to kill and destroy. Why? Because you are empty, each of us needs God's love in our hearts. There is so much to love in a person to give without any connection with sex. Let us discover many more things within our wives, husbands, and others to love them without any sexual thoughts. Please take quality time and examine the life of your spouse or fiancé, and you will discover so much more that is in them to offer other than sexual pleasure?

Love is not something that anyone can see or touch because love cannot be seen because it is spiritual, but the manifestation of love is all around us daily. We can see, feel, and touch love, but many of us cannot see or touch them because we are blind to love. Let's put it this way, you can see it, but your mindset is somewhere else; therefore, you cannot recognize love staring you in the face. Love is so powerful that we can feel it. Love is so deep that, at times, it cannot be expressed in words. Love is so powerful that many have died from a broken heart. Many have become so possessive and extremely jealous and have killed because of love. Love is so strong that it can cause a bonding in a relationship to fuse each other in the hard times and the bad, and they survive. True love can withstand any pressure, hardship, good times, rough times, hills, and valleys, but the couples or individuals must be committed to loving one another. *Please read 1ˢᵗ Corinthians Ch. 13, which contains the following.*

## 1.  *Charity, which is Love suffereth long:*

Therefore, **love is patient,** and when we love someone, we should have patience with them, knowing that we also need others to have patience with us, just as Almighty God is patient with us even when we are doing wrong or don't get it right. Therefore, in the group of the fruit of the Spirit is **Longsuffering, also,** one of the characteristics in *1ˢᵗ Corinthians 13:4* stated that love is **Patient.** Love does not hurry, but it way patiently. Therefore, you and I must be patient with all those that we love because we do not all get to the finish line simultaneously as others.

## 2.  *Love is kind:*

Telling someone that you love them is all good, and it is expected of us to love one another according to the scripture, but that is not enough. Love is a noun, but the characteristic of love can be considered as a verb, an action word; love will cause you to show kindness from the heart, not like some of us, who will give something or help someone and then broadcast it to the world, love does not do such a thing.

Love is not unkind to anyone, regardless of who they are or where they are from, but rather, love is compassionate. Love does not speak harshly to anyone, remembering how our Lord Jesus speaks softly to us. Love is not proud, but rather it embraces others to excel like oneself. Also, love encourages others. Love shows kindness by sharing what you have with others when they do not have it. Love does not have a secret bank account, which would be unkind to your spouse.

**3. *Envieth not:* Envieth,** The *Discontented desire for someone else's possessions or advantage.*

Love does not make you jealous of other people's things. On the contrary, genuine love for people will make you go out of your way to help others achieve for themselves. For example, love does not make you jealous of someone else educational achievements, or their job, their children's accomplishments, their house, vehicles, and so much more.

However, when someone is envious, they are depressed or unhappy because whenever they see you, it reminds them who you are, and they are not, also, to whom you belong or what you possess. It is just like a smile; it takes so much energy to make up your face than it takes to smile; that's what I learn through knowledge. An envious person has a wicked heart, and they can become jealous of you because everything you have, they think it should be them. Love is not envious, love is always kind, and if you are not bearing this fruit, you need to go and meet Jesus. Not having this fruit-bearing in your life is not healthy for your physical health and spiritual condition. Envy can cause someone to hurt others in ways that will be destructive. Deliverance is available at the altar of God for this condition.

**4.  Charity Vaunteth Not Itself: Vaunteth** *To Boast.*

Many people love to boast about themselves even when it is a lie; this is called self-deceit. Many of us brag about our achievements to put others down and to make them feel as if they are inferior to us. Many spouses selfishly use this to belittle their spouses. What do we mean? Some spouses have an excellent educational background; they have achieved their degree; congratulation, we give God thanks for your achievements. However, it is never good to throw your achievement into your spouse's face that may not reach their goal as you are just because there is a misunderstanding in the relationship. Do not remind your spouse, especially women, that you earn more money than him, and you then say he is not the man he supposes to be. Be careful how you are exalting yourself because you can easily fall off your mountaintop.

Suppose you have to boast, boast in the goodness of the Lord Jesus Christ in your life and what He has done for you and your family and continue doing, and not in yourself. Then, if you persist and cannot handle your achievements, pride will set in, and pride is a destroyer for many, just like Satan, the Devil.

**5.  Is Not Puffed up: Puffed,** *Forceful discharge, as of smoke or air. To swell or appear to swell. To inflate with pride or conceit. To praise advertise extravagantly.*

This is what happens to Satan, the Devil; he puffed up in pride. He wanted to be like God, the LORD, and we know what happens according to the scriptures because of pride. Lucifer, who is now named Satan, was expelled from heaven by the God who created him with such beauty, **Ezekiel 28: 12-15.** Many people are puffed up frequently in their pride, be very careful because the fall can be painful. Many are trying to be something or someone and are not, thinking they are better than you and me, just because of their achievement and they have acquired more or become successful in whatever they are doing. This behavior is not true love; it is just selfish pride. Puffed up, also referred to as a big head! "Many people landed and have not yet taken off." be very careful of the fall that may happen.

### 6.  *Do not behave itself unseemly: Improper: unbecoming*

True love does not cause a person to disrespect their spouse or others. True love does not cause you to act like a tyrant. Love does not parade itself in public, bringing shame and disgrace to self and others. (Some people do not have any shame at all for themself, this means that they can shame and disgrace you at will without being embarrassed themself.) Love is not bitter but always gives off a sweet essence. Love is forgiving!

### 7.  *Seeketh not her own:*

True love causes you to be a helper to others and not in a single-minded way. True love will cause you to go out of your way to help others. Love compromise for peace, never resentful or easily irritated of others. The sincerity of love drives you to make sacrifices for your spouse and children and others. Love looks out for others and works behind the scene without popularity.

### 8.  *It is not easily provoked: Provoke: To cause to be irritated or angry. To incite to action.*

True love is patient and not quickly irritated or easily angry for the slightest thing because there is a lack of patience. Instead, you quickly lash out at others in anger to cause hurt. True love does not look for a fight, quarrel, or cause someone to be unhappy.

### 9. *Thinketh no evil:*

True love does not think evil against another person to hurt them. True love does not assassinate someone to gain wealth or possession. Love does not pretend to love, but the fruit of love is harmless and gentle. Love does not harbor death and curses towards others in the heart. True love does not plan another person's downfall and unhappiness when someone is hurting or experiencing pain from this present life on the earth.

The above words mention is the recipe from God the Lord about the actual condition of love. These are just some of the characteristics of a person who truly loves someone other than themselves. Love has no color attached to itself; it does not keep prejudice in the heart. True love does not discriminate against one another in whatever ways it may be. True love does not have limitations, even though sometimes it has to be exercised. True love is from God, our heavenly Father, and Jesus Christ, His Only-begotten Son. God gave His Son, Jesus Christ, this love to give us, and He proved true love for humanity on the cross at Calvary. True love is kind and patient and must be cultivated to bring fort fruit of the Spirit so that it will remain within you even when you are no more; it will speak well of you. If you do not have love, you certainly cannot give or show love. The love of God for all humanity must be in you growing every day so that whenever the fruit of love needs to be displayed, you don't need to go and purchase it or find it, but it should already store up within your heart, ready to give away freely.

**Rejoiceth not in iniquity, but rejoiceth in the truth.**

Until you and I have the true love of God within us, we will be miserable people, looking for something that you cannot find. Love the Lord God and His Son Jesus Christ. Love the Holy Spirit and love yourself; then, you will be able to love others. Therefore, ask God to empty your heart or remove the hate that is within you, and fill you with His love, so that you can be like His Son Jesus Christ, who loves all mankind, regardless of where they come from, who their parents are, rich or poor, sinners and save alike because He possesses love. **Why can't we be like Jesus?**

# CHAPTER SIX

## *Marriage and Divorce:*

As you have been told before, and again we will remind all nations, tongues, and creeds wherever you are, according to the scripture, marriage is of the Lord our God who art in heaven. This remarkable institution did not come from man; instead, it is of the Lord. We are just carrying out the works of God that He has established in heaven so that His will be done on earth as in heaven. When we align ourselves to God's will, His perfect will, will come to pass and will be seen in our daily lives as our fore-parents used to enjoy the Almighty God presence. However, when we do not live in God's **perfect** will, His will now become **permissive,** meaning that the Lord allows you to live your life according to the free will that He has given us. No longer are we guided by the Lord, but we are now following self and others; nevertheless, God extended His tender mercies so that we will not destroy ourselves. As soon as we yield to the Lord Jesus Christ, His will quickly become our will, and now **God's will** be done in our lives as He has planned it to be. As soon as we line up and start to follow Jesus Christ, we will see a significant change in our lives. The completeness of God's plan for humankind is not yet been fulfilled, but in His time and His alone, it shall be done, but until then, we must **Trust** and **Obey** Him and Him alone.

Let us study the word of God together by the Spirit of the Lord and not of the flesh. According to the flesh, we developed selfish desires to please ourselves to justify our ungodly behaviors. Almighty God is not a God of confusion, but Satan is. Remember this about our

God, He is a loving and forgiving God, and when we sin, all we need to do is ask Him to forgive us, and He will. Almighty God loves all of us because we are all His children, children yes, we are all His children; however, not all of God's children know who their heavenly Father is and where He dwells.

**Children:** Yes, all of humanity is God's children, no doubt about that, but not all are God's spiritual children who have accepted Jesus Christ as their Lord and Savior. Many refused to have a relationship with their heavenly Father through their ignorance, but regardless, He still loves all of us. We need to be true to ourselves; not all of us will reign with the Son of God, Jesus Christ because not everyone loves God's Son Jesus Christ, and in Him is everlasting life, and it is for all those who will accept Jesus Christ as their Lord and Savior. Will you receive Him in your life today? If you will, get your Bible and read **Romans 10:8-10**

### 1 Corinthians 14:33 (KJV)

*$^{33}$ For God is not the author of confusion, but of peace, as in all churches of the saints.*

**Notes:** Marriage is between a man and a woman, and it is the **perfect will** of Almighty God. Being married and having children is also the **perfect will** of the Almighty God. However, children born out of wedlock is not, and cannot be God's perfect will; instead, it is God's permissive will. Divorce is not the **Almighty God's perfect will**, except for the only **permission** that Jesus gave, and that is the only condition that one should divorce his wife according to the scripture. However, you should not remarry when you divorce your wife or husband. The scripture below provides us with the purpose of divorce; other than that, we have not seen it mentioned in any other scriptures where the Father **"GOD"** or the Son **"Jesus Christ"** permitted us to divorce our wife or husband. According to the scripture, there is a law concerning marriage, and only death can and should break this law.

### Matthew 5:31-32 (KJV)

*31 It hath been said, Whosoever shall put away his wife, let him give her a writing of divorcement:*

*32 But I say unto you, That whosoever shall put away his wife, saving for the cause of fornication, causeth her to commit adultery: and whosoever shall marry her that is divorced committeth adultery.*

The vows that couples have taken before the Lord and each other stated that they would not leave each other and dissolve the marriage till death do us part, then what has happened? Why are we experiencing so much divorce yearly? It is not acceptable to divorce your spouse because it was never God's plan for humanity to separate themselves from each other when married except by death. Even though Moses permitted the children of Israel to put away "divorce" their wives, it was never God's **perfect will** for couples' "spouses" to be separated from each other through a divorce. But it was because of the hardness, the Adamic sinful nature manifesting itself in those people's hearts, and even now, we are no better than those before us because we are still rebelling against God's commandment concerning marriage. When Moses permitted them to write a bill of divorcement, which they did, please remember, it was never God's perfect plan for them and us. From then to this present time, people are still divorcing each other because of their self-will, and it will continue because we do not regard God's instructions. Remember, it was because of their fleshly desires to satisfy themselves and not God.

### *This is the scripture:*

### Matthew 19:7-8 (KJV)

*7 They say unto him, Why did Moses then command to give a writing of divorcement, and to put her away?*

*⁸ He saith unto them, Moses because of the hardness of your hearts suffered you to put away your wives: but from the beginning it was not so.*

**Notes:** Now, when Jesus gave the only example for divorce, there is nowhere else in the scriptures that mention for us to remarry. God is God, and He does not have twisted tongues like some of us, say one thing and mean another. The scripture told us that God is not a man that He should lie; therefore, whatever the LORD God said, it is exactly what He means, nothing more and nothing less. The written word of Almighty God is what we have here in this world to guide us in our spiritual walk with Jesus, and we must take His words seriously. Jesus did many things we know not of but said that the Holy Spirit would teach us and reveal those things through revelations, and the Spirit is truth.

## These are the scripture:

### John 21:25 (KJV)

*²⁵ And there are also many other things which Jesus did, the which, if they should be written every one, I suppose that even the world itself could not contain the books that should be written. Amen.*

### Numbers 23:19 (KJV)

*¹⁹ God is not a man, that he should lie; neither the son of man, that he should repent: hath he said, and shall he not do it? or hath he spoken, and shall he not make it good?*

**Notes:** Before we get into the sound doctrine of the scriptures that speak about divorce, we need to understand that God does not change. He is still the same God that was in the Old Testament. Therefore, no matter how many excuses we may give for some of our decisions to justify our behavior, do what you want to do, but it does not change, or will it ever change what Almighty God has already said. However, there is a verse that we need to consider carefully because the Lord does not want anyone of us to burn in our lust and die and end up in hell. Whatever you decide to do in remarrying, go to God your Father in heaven in prayer and get instruction from Him about getting married again. Or, ask Him to forgive you for remarrying even though His word said that you should not, and He is a loving God ready to forgive.

## 1ˢᵗ Corinthians 7

## Corinthians7:1(KJV)

*¹ Now concerning the things whereof ye wrote unto me:
It is good for a man not to touch a woman.*

**Notes:** The Corinthians were troubled and needed a better clarification about marriage and divorce, and several other things in chapter seven, so the Apostle Paul addresses the question in **1ˢᵗ Corinthians 7**

It is always good to be married because we do not believe that God wants us to be alone. The Lord God did not allow Adam to be alone without someone like himself, except for those men who were not given to marriage, as stated in **Matthew 19:12.** Therefore, verse one says; it is not good for any man to touch a woman without being married to her.

Let us study further; in **Genesis 1:28,** according to God's instruction and the principle of the Holy God, it should never happen except by marriage because we can only multiply and *replenish* the earth legally under the law of God; why? Because sexual intercourse out of wedlock is a sin, and God would not encourage anyone of us to break His law. We believe that the first verse interpretation has given us an understanding of sexual practices between men and women.

According to God's word, no one has the legal right from the Lord to be intimate in a sexual relationship with the opposite sex without being married to that person.

### 1ˢᵗ Corinthians 7:2 (KJV)

*² Nevertheless, to avoid fornication, let every man have his own wife, and let every woman have her own husband.*

### 1ˢᵗ Corinthians 6:18

*¹⁸ Flee fornication. Every sin that a man doeth is without the body; but he that committeth fornication sinneth against his own body.*

**Notes:** To avoid sinning against God and your own body, **1ˢᵗ Corinthians 7:2** inform us of such. Also, **1ˢᵗ Corinthians 6: 18** verify that when we practice fornication, we sin against God and our own body. Therefore, each man must have his own wife. Each woman must have her own husband because when any one of us sleeps with another person that does not belong to us, you and I are also breaking the law of God by committing adultery and fornication. When a married person sleeps with another married person, they have committed adultery.

When two unmarried people have sexual intercourse, they commit fornication. When a married person and a single person have sexual intercourse, one commits adultery and the other fornication. Therefore, as the scripture said, let every man have his own wife and the woman have her own husband so that none will sin against God and their own body.

Again, these two behaviors are a sin, according to the scripture. Furthermore, the married spouse has defiled their marriage bed.

### Exodus 20:14 (KJV)

### Thou shalt not commit adultery.

**Notes:** Not only do we commit adultery because of our actions, but we have disrespected our spouses and dishonored them because of the act that we have done. The scripture below tells us that any person who does this defiles the marriage bed. Therefore, when anyone violates the marriage bed, that person is not wise.

### Proverbs 6:29 (KJV)

*29 So he that goeth in to his neighbour's wife; whosoever toucheth her shall not be innocent.*

### Proverbs 6:32 (KJV)

*32 But whoso committeth adultery with a woman lacketh understanding: he that doeth it destroyeth his own soul.*

### 1st Corinthians 7:3 (KJV)

*3 Let the husband render unto the wife due benevolence: and likewise also the wife unto the husband.*

**Notes:** Each person in the marriage relationship must show kindness to each other no matter what differences both may have towards one another. Each person must support one another in affection, at no time neglecting your spouse's needs for any selfish reason to please yourself. The husband or wife should never allow Satan to tempt any one of them because the marital relationship is experiencing stress in the marriage at this time. Whatever is going on wrong in the relationship, no matter the reason, it does not and should never cause one to sleep with someone other than their spouse. That is not showing kindness but revenge. The husband or wife should not withdraw from each other, neglecting themselves from comforting each other, so Satan does not come in and entice them to someone else. By not satisfying each other's needs, they can allow lust to set in and then go astray. Each other must surrender themselves to one another for the sake of unity and to resist the devil so that he will take a flight out of your life, home, and marriage. Do not be unkind to each other because of your carelessness; when Satan leaves you, he does not leave you for good; he is just taking time out planning a more wicked plan to come back at you. Therefore, be ye sober, vigilant, and always praying to God in heaven in Jesus' precious name. Be always kind to each other in giving and sharing yourself and things with one another, knowing what the word of God has said about being benevolent, showing kindness.

### 1st Corinthians7:4(KJV)

[4] The wife hath not power of her own body, but the husband: and likewise also the husband hath not power of his own body, but the wife.

**Notes:** The husband or wife does not have power over his or her own body unequally. According to the scripture, the husband should not say to his wife that he controls her body, but she does not have power over him. Neither can he claim that she does not have control over his body. Again, the scripture is telling us clearly to our most straightforward understanding. Each other have the same power or authority over one another's body. It would be unfair if any spouse demands complete control over the other and refuses to submit under the same power. The husband cannot require his wife to completely surrender herself to him while refusing to surrender himself unto her in the same manner; if that should happen, it is hypocrisy. Please remember what the scripture clearly states about the husband and the wife having power; it concerns their body.

God is a wise God, full of knowledge and wisdom. He is a God of peace and not war; therefore, he required both husband and wife to have equal authority over each other's body for the marriage to be balanced. None of the spouses should do whatever they please with their body without regard for the other. The wife should not deny her husband of herself that would cause him to turn to any form of sexual immoralities such as pornography on electronic media, magazines, movies, and more; all these are sins. The husband is to do the same for his wife so that there will be a godly balance.

### 1st Corinthians 7:5 (KJV)

⁵ Defraud ye not one the other, except *it be* with consent for a time, that ye may give yourselves to fasting and prayer; and come together again, that Satan tempt you not for your incontinency.

**Notes:** Many may have other interpretations about this verse, but we believe that this verse is informing all of us, the married couple, that the only time that you should restrain yourself from sexual intercourse with each other and only during this time as stated by scripture is when one or both are giving themselves unto the Lord in fasting and prayer. During this time, the spouse should restrain themselves from sexual intercourse with consent because they have given themselves unto the Lord God in service. Although denying oneself from the pleasure of the flesh or sexual desire for the Lord is an excellent service, the Lord does honor your sacrifice.

The scripture clearly stated it to be so; however, the scripture again said this; do not hesitate for too long after giving one's self to the Lord to come together quickly before lust enters the heart, because Satan will use it to tempt you, in thoughts, and deeds. Couples do not ever use sex as a weapon against each other as many has done and are still doing to their spouse; this is folly and wickedness. Sex is not an object of a weapon for war in a relationship to display revenge because of some form of misunderstanding. For the sake of peace in Jesus' name who suffered and died for us, do not allow the carnal mind enter your heart and sin and die in your sin for what, over foolishness.

**1ˢᵗ Corinthians 7:6 (KJV)**

*⁶But I speak this by permission, and not of commandment.*

**Notes:** We believe that the Apostle Paul is referring this verse to the following verses. Also, the Apostle Paul was honest. Can you see his honesty? He said it is not by divine commandment, but he speaks or states the below verses by permission.

**1ˢᵗ Corinthians 7:7-9 (KJV)**

*⁷ For I would that all men were even as I myself. But every man hath his proper gift of God, one after this manner, and another after that.*

**1ˢᵗ *Corinthians 7:8 (KJV)***

***⁸ I say therefore to the unmarried and widows, It is good for them if they abide even as I.***

**Notes:** The Apostle Paul was a single man, and he is making the statement that it is okay if you will be like him, but if you can't be like him, you ought to get married. Verse eight (8) be as I am. In what state was the Apostle Paul? He was not married. But if you cannot be like me, Paul, then get married because it is better to get married than burn in your lust and then die in your sins and end up in hell. It is better to marry than to be single and burn in your lustful desire. However, we must seek the face of the Lord so that He will direct you what to do because His word still stands about a husband or a wife entering into divorcing each other.

A crucial point in verse eight that we need to understand is that the Apostle Paul was not speaking to married people; instead, the reference is towards singles. Therefore, as stated, if you are married and, in a divorce, try and work it out in the Lord, and it will take you praying to the Lord who will work in the heart of the spouse who is the trouble maker in the marriage. However, if none of you are willing to work on your relationship to please the Lord Jesus, then you need to go and repent unto Him, and state your case and hear what He has to say. But remember, if you are willing to set asunder, know this, you must not remarry according to the scripture. Therefore, go and work out your problems and strengthen your relationship, see whatever went wrong, work on it and make it right again, and this time, do not abuse each other.

### 1ˢᵗ Corinthians 7:10 (KJV)

¹⁰ And unto the married I command, *yet* not I, but
the Lord, Let not the wife depart from *her* husband:

**Notes:** Verse ten, the Apostle Paul was no longer under permission but under direct commandment from the Lord to share to us the **perfect will** of God. He is speaking to married couples, a man and a woman. Paul tells us clearly that he is not the one who is now speaking to us, the couples, but it is the Lord our God. Now we are getting into the substance of marriage and divorce. You may not like what the Lord is about to say to us, but whether you or I like it or not, the word of God stands. Before we go further here this,

### Psalm 119:89 (KJV)

⁸⁹ *For ever, O LORD, thy word is settled in heaven.*

**Notes:** Wives, you are not to depart (**walkout/divorce**) from your husband for no reason whatsoever, except for only one reason that the Lord Jesus gave. You have no legal right from the Lord to do so. It is never God's **perfect** will for any couple to enter into separation because the Lord does not want us to be contentious and unruly. Separation is division, and division brings fort confusion, and confusion brings fort chaos, and these behaviors are of the devil.

We know that some relationships are very toxic and cause the atmosphere in the home to smell very severely. The smell we are referring to is hate, bitterness, strife, quarrels and bickering, cheating on your spouse, and infidelity causes many wives to walk out on their husbands. Emotionally, we understand, but we must remember that we have to answer to God for our decisions in this world. Every day, Wives pray for your husband, for prayer does work when you reach out to God in heaven. Then, He, the Lord, will take control of his heart and turn his mindset of love towards God and you. Why God? If your husband did love God, he would not be treating you, his wife, in such a manner because he would obey the Lord, but he has given himself to the spirit of disobedience. God has commanded the husband to love his wife as His Son, Jesus Christ, loved us and died for all of us.

Many of us think that we can change a person heart from evil or from doing wrong, but it is sad to say, you and I cannot do such, it is God and God alone who knows the heart of mankind, and He is the only **One** whom we need to ask to make such change. Yes, we can counsel others and help redirect them into the right path to make the correct decisions in life, but to change people, we cannot. Therefore, through prayer, we pray to God in heaven in Jesus Christ's precious name for the Lord God to turn human hearts from wickedness and evil thoughts to righteousness. This is because our Father in heaven created humanity and made us in His image and after His likeness says about the heart's conditions.

**Jeremiah 17:9-10 (KJV)**

*[9] The heart is deceitful above all things, and desperately wicked: who can know it?*

*[10] I the LORD search the heart, I try the reins, even to give every man according to his ways, and according to the fruit of his doings.*

So, you see, marrying a person hoping that they will change is not the solution to your problems. You need to get in touch with the problem-solver, and His name is Jesus. He is never too busy to listen to your call. Jesus already knows of you and about you. He is waiting for you to make that call; please call on Him now, and file a complaint to the heavenly court in prayer concerning your husband. Also, singles are welcome to seek the Lord Jesus in prayer for the person that will one day be your spouse. Please do not wait until marriage to pray; pray now that the Lord God in Jesus precious name will fix both of you for you. We need to make more sensible or careful decisions because marriage is not just for that day of excitement or few years as many may think, but it is until deaths do both of you part in Jesus Christ's precious name. Therefore, know whom you will marry; if they are jealous now, they will be super jealous after the wedding.

If they are miserable now, they will be super-miserable after the wedding because now it may conceive in their mind that you are now theirs and they are currently licensed to treat you any and anyhow. After all, you are now there's. So, stop and listen to the voice of God and obey Him when He speaks to you. Please accept our deepest sympathy for the sorrows that you are experiencing from your spouse or finance. Some wives are experiencing a horrible married life; some call it hell, no peace, no love as they are going through this hellish experience on this earth because some husbands refuse to obey the Lord's commandment in the way they ought to treat their wife.

According to the scripture, the wife has no legal right to walk out from her home and away from her husband, and if you choose to do so, the next verse tells you what you must do and cannot do. Yes, humanity will tell you differently, and we are always quick to listen to them rather than God. Whose report do you or we believe? Please do not wait until trouble comes home, be on the offensive in prayer, don't wait until you are in danger to remember God in prayer.

**1 Corinthians 7:11 (KJV)**

*<sup>11</sup> But and if she depart, let her remain unmarried, or be reconciled to her husband: and let not the husband put away his wife.*

**Notes:** If the wife departs, meaning to walk out (being separated, or divorce) of the marriage, she must not get married to another man; she ought to stay married yet single because she has no legal grounds to divorce her husband and marry another man. She is not at liberty to marry again; she is to remain unmarried, or reconcile to her husband, meaning, go and make up with her husband. Wives, your answer to your dilemma is prayer and fasting; pray, and when you pray, pray some more, and seek godly counsel. Please remember that our Father in heaven does not like a broken home.

The husband is not to put away his wife, meaning he must not divorce his wife for any reason other than the one given by the Lord Jesus Christ. The husband has no legal right to divorce his wife because they fall out of love; well, go and fall back into it. Also, as mentioned before, the wife is not to put away her husband. According to the scripture, if the wife decides to leave her husband, she must stay unmarried or reconcile. Why? Because God said it to be so, He hateth putting away, the husband has no authority from God, our Father, to put away his wife for any other reason, again, other than the same that the Lord Jesus Christ gave, and that is the only reason.

## These are the scriptures:

**Malachi 2:14-16 (KJV)**

*<sup>14</sup> Yet ye say, Wherefore? Because the LORD hath been witness between thee and the wife of thy youth, against whom thou hast dealt treacherously: yet is she thy companion, and the wife of thy covenant.*

*¹⁵ And did not he make one? Yet had he the residue of the spirit. And wherefore one? That he might seek a godly seed. Therefore take heed to your spirit, and let none deal treacherously against the wife of his youth.*

*¹⁶ For the LORD, the God of Israel, saith that he hateth putting away: for one covereth violence with his garment, saith the LORD of hosts: therefore take heed to your spirit, that ye deal not treacherously.*

## Matthew 5:31-32 (KJV)

*³¹ It hath been said, Whosoever shall put away his wife, let him give her a writing of divorcement:*

*³² But I say unto you, That whosoever shall put away his wife, saving for the cause of fornication, causeth her to commit adultery: and whosoever shall marry her that is divorced committeth adultery.*

## Notes: Malachi

What the Lord is telling us in Malachi is this, that it is wicked of any man to marry the wife of his youth, and then later he dealt with her treacherously by putting her away, "divorce her." In the wisdom of God, it is not suitable for any man to do such a thing. Marriage is not a contract as many of us have thought it to be; instead, it is a covenant between the husband and his wife because the Lord God is a witness to the marriage, not only those who have attended the wedding. Again, we can see that when two people get married, they are one, the Lord cause us to be one so that they may have children from the marriage and the scripture will be fulfilled as it is written in the book of **Genesis 1:28,** that mankind should replenish the earth. We are warned that none of us should deal treacherously with our wife; let us learn from the word of God and live in peace for Christ sake.

## *Continue:*

Jesus says that when a husband divorces his wife other than fornication, he causes her to commit adultery with her new husband. The new husband also commits adultery because he marries a woman that belongs to another man. Why? The law of divorce is still in effect for her and him. Please continue reading to have a better understanding of how the Lord takes the relationship in marriage seriously. Do not be upset about your life that you are a mistake; people's heart is very deceitful; we say one thing and mean another. That's why sometimes it causes some people not to have confidence in relationships. Don't allow other people's problems to be yours; instead, learn from their mistakes.

### Proverbs 6:32 (KJV)

*32 But whoso committeth adultery with a woman lacketh understanding: he that doeth it destroyeth his own soul.*

## Notes:

### *The word putting away means divorce.*

While the Lord Jesus was on the earth, He taught the people to live a righteous and holy life to please the Father who art in heaven. He teaches them the correct way, and as we read the Bible, we are also being taught the right way to live our lives upon the earth. Therefore, when human beings follow the instruction from the prescribed medicine of the word given to us by Doctor Jesus, the Great Physician, through the inspiration of the Holy Spirit, we will please the Father and inherit eternal life, and this life is in Jesus Christ.

God, our heavenly Father, always speaks to us when we read His Word in the Holy Bible, even though many people have rejected the Bible because they don't want to conform to spiritual change. The

Lord God speaks against living a life of sin, and to follow Jesus Christ doing good, each person will have to give up many things of the world because the things of the world are enmity "enemy" of God.

Now we know through the written word of God, according to the scripture above, when a man marries a woman and becomes his wife, the husband has no legal right to divorce his wife except for fornication. Again, if that husband disobeys God's law and divorces his wife and she marries another man, she commits adultery, again according to the scripture. The husband also commits adultery if he remarries because the divorced wife is still considered married under God's Universal Law of marriage. It seems unfair, or maybe not right, but remember, it is God's words and not ours. By the way, this should teach all of us that we must love our spouse and know that we will live with each other until death and stop nagging one another over foolishness so that peace will remain.

### Matthew 19:3-9 (KJV)

*³ The Pharisees also came unto him, tempting him, and saying unto him, Is it lawful for a man to put away his wife for every cause?*

*⁴ And he answered and said unto them, Have ye not read, that he which made them at the beginning made them male and female,*

*⁵ And said, For this cause shall a man leave father and mother, and shall cleave to his wife: and they twain shall be one flesh?*

*⁶ Wherefore they are no more twain, but one flesh. What therefore God hath joined together, let not man put asunder.*

*⁷ They say unto him, Why did Moses then command to give a writing of divorcement, and to put her away?*

*⁸ He saith unto them, Moses because of the hardness of your hearts suffered you to put away your wives: but from the beginning it was not so.*

*⁹ And I say unto you, Whosoever shall put away his wife, except it be for fornication, and shall marry another, committeth adultery: and whoso marrieth her which is put away doth commit adultery.*

## Notes:

In the above verses, the Lord Jesus teaches us, both in the past and now in the present time, that our heavenly Father, the Lord God, made human beings from the ***beginning.*** Adam and Eve, male and female, and that's how God ordains it to be, and that's how we must keep it and never change any word to satisfy our fleshly desires. We are not like some politicians who speak lies in truth to fool people to please the masses. We read the word of God and said, "**Thy will be done on earth as in heaven**" well, it is God's will; therefore, let His will be done on the earth by not divorcing our spouses just because, just because what? You don't love her anymore, well, go and stir up the fire of love again, and love her and show her love; the same goes to the wife. God does not like broken marriages. What if He should divorce us from being one of His creations? We would not have a heavenly Father who cares for us and to save us from hellfire. For all those who are not yet married, please make sure that you are ready spiritually, financially, emotionally, mentally, and physically so that you and yours can have a successful life in your marriage and relationship.

The **perfect** will of God for us besides worshipping Him the Lord is that we will get married, bear children, and for us to love each other and live in peace with one another for the rest of our lives. When a man marries a woman, they are no longer two separate people in the eyes of God, even though they have two individual bodies. They are now joined together as one person through marriage, and this is the perfect will of the Lord. Again, marriage is a beautiful institution established and blessed by the Lord God. Through marriage, the Lord uses this spiritual and sacred event to bring man and woman back together as He has them from the beginning. In the beginning, Eve "Woman" was in man "Adam," God took her out from man, but for God to have man and woman back together, He does it through marriage. Isn't this great? Only the Highest, the God of creations, can do such a wonderful and glorious thing. But besides all of that, God wants our obedience to Him; failure to obey, His will cannot be done on earth.

Also, a significant fact about marriage and keeping ourselves with each other cut down on sexually transmitted diseases. However, when we go outside of the marriage union and start sleeping around with others, it is possible to bring home diseases to your spouse, and if your spouse is doing the same thing, that spouse, in turn, gives it to someone else and that someone else gives it to their spouse. This entire sexual escapade, now we see how **STDs** get around. Please, let us all stay clean and safe, join together with our spouse, and live a long healthy life as God will allow.

No man has the authority to pass a law giving us the right to divorce our spouse whenever we choose; if things are not working out the way we plan it well, go and plan it again and fix it. So do not allow the devil to control your life; let us all obey God by His word and not the terms of men so that we can satisfy our fleshly desires.

God said we must leave father and mother and cleave to each other, being two, yet we are one. Also, we must not allow anyone to untie or lose what God has joined together, but some of us are unlearned when it comes to the word of God for humanity, and some of us do not care if it is God or man; they are going to do what pleases themselves. When we do not obey and follow instructions from our heavenly Father, there will be consequences, and when it comes, we begin to blame others. Therefore, husband and wife, do not allow

Satan to harden each of your hearts to go contrary to what God said you should not do.

### John 14:23-24 (KJV)

*²³ Jesus answered and said unto him, If a man love me, he will keep my words: and my Father will love him, and we will come unto him, and make our abode with him.*

*²⁴ He that loveth me not keepeth not my sayings: and the word which ye hear is not mine, but the Father's which sent me.*

Again, we can see the Lord Jesus speaketh, teaching us in the scriptures that the Father of all living does not approve of anyone writing a bill of divorcement from the beginning of time. But Moses, because of the hardness of the heart through the pressuring of the people back then, Moses permitted them that they could divorce their wives. Jesus came and made things clear for us by explaining how the LORD feels about separation. However, it was never God's plan for humanity to separate themselves from each other after marriage since He hateth putting away. Jesus gave us a better understanding of marriage and divorce. Mankind's view does not always line up or represent heaven's point of view because it may be legal on paper on the earth but cannot be found in the book of heaven.

### Isaiah 55:6-11 (KJV)

*⁶ Seek ye the LORD while he may be found, call ye upon him while he is near:*

*⁷ Let the wicked forsake his way, and the unrighteous man his thoughts: and let him return unto the LORD, and he will have mercy upon him; and to our God, for he will abundantly pardon.*

*⁸ For my thoughts are not your thoughts, neither are your ways my ways, saith the LORD.*

*⁹ For as the heavens are higher than the earth, so are my ways higher than your ways, and my thoughts than your thoughts.*

*¹⁰ For as the rain cometh down, and the snow from heaven, and returneth not thither, but watereth the earth, and maketh it bring forth and bud, that it may give seed to the sower, and bread to the eater:*

*¹¹ So shall my word be that goeth forth out of my mouth: it shall not return unto me void, but it shall accomplish that which I please, and it shall prosper in the thing whereto I sent it.*

## 1 Corinthians 7:12 (KJV)

*¹² But to the rest speak I, not the Lord: If any brother hath a wife that believeth not, and she be pleased to dwell with him, let him not put her away.*

## Notes:

Once again, the Apostle Paul is honest to us; he is telling us that what he is about to say is not from the Lord Jesus, but he is the one who is giving his spiritual advice through permission. He tells us that if a saved man has a wife who is not born of the Spirit, the born-again husband should not put her away "divorce" his unsaved wife, but they two should live in peace for the sake of the marriage to please God our heavenly Father.

**1 Corinthians 7:13 (KJV)**

*13 And the woman which hath an husband that believeth not, and if he be pleased to dwell with her, let her not leave him.*

## Notes:

Verse thirteen is the same as verse twelve (12), one is referring to the husband and the wife concerning unsaved spouse, that the saved wife should not put away "divorce" her unsaved husband, but they two should live in peace for the sake of the marriage.

**1 Corinthians 7:14 (KJV)**

*14 For the unbelieving husband is sanctified by the wife, and the unbelieving wife is sanctified by the husband: else were your children unclean; but now are they holy.*

## Note:

Please note the power of God in Christian's lives; how the sanctified husband or wife sanctifies the unbelieving husband or wife. Isn't the Lord great in the things that He does? And as they lived together, the consecrated life of the saved couples that they are living, one day can cause the unsaved person to accept Jesus Christ, and their children will not be considered unclean.

**1 Corinthians 7:15-24 (KJV)**

*15 But if the unbelieving depart, let him depart. A brother or a sister is not under bondage in such cases: but God hath called us to peace.*

*[16] For what knowest thou, O wife, whether thou shalt save thy husband? or how knowest thou,*

**1 Corinthians 7:25-26 (KJV)**

*[25] Now concerning virgins I have no commandment of the Lord: yet I give my judgment, as one that hath obtained mercy of the Lord to be faithful.*

*[26] I suppose therefore that this is good for the present distress, I say, that it is good for a man so to be.*

## Notes:

There are no commandments from the Lord concerning virgins, but the Apostle Paul is giving his recommendations. During that time, there was uncertainty upon the earth in those regions. Getting into marriage would not be good for the virgins because she could become a widow soon after marriage, but the Almighty is always gracious.

Hear the writers' opinion; we believe that when young men or girls keep themselves until they are married, the Lord has a special blessing for them. But these days, many believe that if they don't have sex before marriage, it is not worth it because they do not know how their future spouse will perform in the bedroom. Everything can be well now before getting married and then later on in life, things collapse and your fear before looking at you now, what then?

Sex is essential in marriage, but that does not make the person be who they are because it is the inner person you need to get connected to and not the pleasure that anyone can get through sex.

I guess that many of us have been getting this relationship and marriage wrong. As it has been said, "let get back to the drawing board," renew your mindset.

**1 Corinthians 7:27 (KJV)**

[27] Art thou bound unto a wife? seek not to be loosed. Art thou loosed from a wife? seek not a wife.

## Notes:

Men, if you are married, you are bound or tied to your wife under the law of marriage, and you should not seek to be loosed (do not divorce) yourself from your wife. The same advice is given to the wife as it is given to her husband. Now that you are married men and ladies, husband, you are now spiritually bound to your wife until death do you part, and the wife is also tied to her husband as long as they are alive. Therefore, none of you should seek to be loosed from each other because the Lord says so. Whose report do you believe?

**1 Corinthians 7:39 (KJV)**

[39] The wife is bound by the law as long as her husband liveth; but if her husband be dead, she is at liberty to be married to whom she will; only in the Lord.

**Romans 7:2-3 (KJV)**

[2] For the woman which hath an husband is bound by the law to *her* husband so long as he liveth; but if the husband be dead, she is loosed from the law of *her* husband.

[3] So then if, while *her* husband liveth, she be married to another man, she shall be called an adulteress: but if her husband be dead, she is free from that law; so that she is no adulteress, though she be married to another man.

## Notes:

There is a law of marriage, the law that was established from the beginning by God. From the beginning, God, who is above all other gods, made Adam and Eve male and female, and both were one flesh, as the scripture stated. God has joined them together, and He is still joining people together; let no one in the earth, under the earth, or the prince of the air separate or destroy what Almighty God has ordained. What did God ordain? Of course, He ordains marriage, and marriage is between a man and a woman **ONLY.**

Only death should legally break the true meaning of the law of marriage. If the wife's husband lives, she is still married to him by the law of marriage based upon Almighty God's word, but she is no longer under the law of marriage when he dies. She can remarry anyone she chooses to; however, a born-again person should only marry a spiritually born person. Why? Because the scripture spoke to us about the unequal yoke.

### 2 Corinthians 6:14 (KJV)

*¹⁴ Be ye not unequally yoked together with unbelievers: for what fellowship hath righteousness with unrighteousness? and what communion hath light with darkness?*

It is the same concerning the wife, she is not to divorce her husband, but if her husband is dead, she is free to remarry in the Lord, meaning a saved woman should marry a saved man according to the scripture.

Many of us live our lives out of the perfect will of God, our Father, and as we do so, we live a life of disobedience to Him, and rebellion is sin. Ask your Father in heaven to forgive you for sinning against Him through ignorance, but now that we know what the scripture said about marriage, let us line up and work on our relationship and do not be so quick to end that which you have spent so much time to build.

It is full time we as human beings get back to know our Father God in heaven and live our lives to please Him and Him alone. This information is new to many, but we cannot change what was and will always be. All we can do is go to our Father in heaven and ask Him to forgive us of our sins in Jesus Christ precious name, and now, let all of us follow and do the commandments of Almighty God.

God sanctifies marriage before the foundation of the earth in the spirit; therefore, let us obey the Lord by His word, live in peace, and let us enjoy the union with our spouse. However, because of sin, many relationships and marriages are experiencing severe stress to the point where people live in fear, misery, lack of respect because there is no unity among the spouses. But it is about time that husband and wife come together and put away their pride, selfish behavior and humble themselves before the God of heaven so that you and your spouse can plan for a successful life ahead in Jesus' name.

Also, it is time for the singles to put away selfishness and stubbornness and stop using and abusing each other for your selfish gain in Jesus' name. We are all God's children, and we must learn how to live with each other and among one another. None of us are better than the other, we live and die, and there are no exceptions. We all share the same common denominator, life and death, and after that, the judgment before the living God. So, please, let us all learn to live in peace and allow the love of God to reign in our hearts, not man's love, but God's love.

### *Just a side note:*

This message is for wives; whomever you may be throughout the four corners of the earth, you have chosen to be a housewife. You used to look so good or acceptable before you got married, and now you are married and have children, and you are no longer looking like the person you used to be. We know age changes people's looks, but that is not what we are talking about concerning aging. What happens? You wake up in the morning probably make your husband and children breakfast. I hope that you have taken time out and gotten something to eat? That same house dress you have on before your husband and children leave the house, they come back and find you in the same dress. Why is that? Why haven't you made time and cared for yourself, looking good for you and your husband? Do not let your husband see you as a housemaid and not a wife? There are six days to work and get everything in the house in order.

Your husband may not find you attractive again because you have allowed yourself to run down. So please wake up and do something to your hair, put some facial crème on your face and let it shine again. Husband, since your wife is a housewife, you are responsible for giving her money to go and take care of herself so that she can look pretty for you again instead of complaining.

And many wives work and never find time to take care of themselves. All they do is work and work and develop pain in their body that turns into arthritis. Wives, this is not good; you are working too hard and not smart. After you finish a hard day at work, you have to come home and make dinner for the family; after a while, it can get exhaustive, and very soon, your body gets run down to nothing. Husbands, have a meeting with your wife and see how her duties in the house can be less stressful. For example, you may have to start dinner before she comes home and helps the children with their homework, and depending on their age, you may have to bathe them. House duties are hard work, and it's not for women alone; time has changed where two people in the home are working; therefore, there must be a balance. So, find the balance, take care of yourself, and have a wonderful time by enjoying your relationship and marriage that will please your Lord.

## Where are all the mothers?

According to the scripture in **Titus Ch 2,** it is the older mothers' responsibility to teach young women how to take care of their homes and to love their husbands. I know that it gets tough to correct some young men and ladies in this time that we are living in since people are so sensitive.

Many young ones do not want anyone who is not their parents to correct them because some of them are not properly trained at home; they are rebellious; not even their parents can correct them.

In my days, the older brethren, fathers, and mothers of the church corrected us; even though they were not our parents, we did not like the correction, but we never disrespected them because of who they were to us. But nowadays, it is so difficult because some of the parents of the children will attack you. Things in this world are complicated, and it is not getting any better because humans are far from the Lord.

There was a time in the church we could not be outside while church service was going on, it did not make a difference who that adult was; they would direct you into the building, and then depending on the person, they will report you to your parent/s, and then your parents will pick up from there. So, young adults, please listen! Our parents' words were law then, and they expected us to follow their instructions, but, whether they were right or wrong, they speak, we listen and obey and respect them because of who they were to us, they were and are our parents.

Nowadays, many of our children are taking over the parent's role, and they speak to many of us parents as if they are the adult and we are the child. The Bible says that we, the parent, should and must train our children in the way of the Lord God. We must do all that needs to be done for our children because not everyone will tolerate their disrespectful behavior outside the home. Some of our children have caused premature death upon themselves because of their behavior.

But for the living, there is hope for them because they are alive; parents let us get down on our knees and cry aloud in prayer to God and let Him know the burden of urgency concerning our children before it is too late. Unfortunately, many godly fathers and mothers cannot correct the young ones in the church because they have no respect for the older person. Sometimes, the saved parents are the disrespectful ones attacking one another over foolishness.

Fathers and mothers', let us save all those that can be saved through corrections and pray for them in Jesus's holy name before the devil gets them permanently.

Parents, as you know that our hands are tied with pen and paper from government officials. They passed laws preventing us from training our children the proper way the Lord God has commanded us to do. Can you imagine that if you discipline your children and they don't like it, they can call the authority to get you arrested?

And parents, we must admit, some of these children go out there and terrorize the innocence and even kill authority because they were not under godly discipline since they were young. So, we do not want to be naïve, even though some can get the best training and become a destructive weapon for Satan. The answer to all of our problems on the earth is to accept Jesus Christ as Lord and Savior and love people. Respect self and others. Be kind at all times. Cross over from that side to this side where Jesus is, and your life will be changed knowing that there is life everlasting waiting for you. Why don't you come to Jesus today? Jesus is waiting for you.

We thank all of you for purchasing this book, and we pray that it will be a blessing to you and your family as you enjoy reading the information in this book. May God continue to bless every household as you make the necessary adjustment to live in peace and experience success in your life in Jesus' precious name.

## *To God be the Glory!*

*Many thanks,*

*Pastor Denburk Gregory*
*and*
*Min. Veronica Gregory*

# CHAPTER SEVEN

## Bishop A. Brown Messages:

The following pages are messages from our Bishop of the **Full Truth Church of God Deliverance Center,** *General Overseer,* Bishop Arthur Brown. Church Head Quarter in Kingston 4, Jamaica West Indies. We would like to extend our greetings to the readers from the Full Truth Church of God family. We, the writers, would like to thank each person who purchased this book. We pray that the Lord Jesus Christ will bless everyone and their family as you read the writings of this book and enjoy Bishop Brown and his wife, Pastor B. Brown's spiritual teaching. We try to bring to your home the undiluted word of the living God and His Son Jesus Christ through the power of the Holy Spirit. God richly bless you, and again, please enjoy the following messages from our Bishop.

January 02, 2019

Precious Saints, greetings.

**Topic:** *GIVING PRIORITY TO A GREAT THING OVER A GOOD THING.*

**Text:** Matthew 14:22-23

"JESUS SENT THE MULTITUDES AWAY, AND THEN WENT UP INTO THE MOUNTAIN APART TO PRAY."

**Introduction:**

Most of us would not have done what Jesus did. We love to be with the crowd. We would have seized the GOOD OPPORTUNITY to convert the thousands and spent the night baptizing them. Instead, Jesus seized the GREAT OPPORTUNITY to spend the night in the mountain in PRAYER.

Let's examine some things about this very huge crowd.

1.  They DELIBERATELY followed Jesus for miles on foot from THE CITY TO A DESERT PLACE. **Ch 14:13.**

    They were not coincidental bystanders. They were people with a mission and purpose.

2.  Many were GLORIOUSLY healed by Jesus. **V14.** Their needs were MIRACULOUSLY met.

3.  They were ALL SUMPTUOUSLY fed by Jesus. **Verse 20** says, "THEY DID ALL EAT, AND WERE FILLED."

4.  They APPRECIATIVELY wanted to make Jesus A KING. **St John 6:15.**

This crowd was not UNGRATEFUL like the TEN LEPERS who refused to tell Jesus THANKS. Instead, They were ready to crown Jesus as their KING. Most preachers would love to have these types of members, YET JESUS SENT THEM AWAY.

**Conclusion:**

It was at this moment of EARTHLY EXALTATION that Jesus DISMISSED the crowd in order to ASCEND THE MOUNTAIN OF PRAYER TO RECEIVE HEAVENLY EXALTATION.

When the PROGRAMME takes PRIORITY over PRAYER, the PEOPLE suffer PERILOUSLY.

Jesus did them greater good than harm by sending them away. Jesus went away to receive POWER TO TEACH, PREACH AND HEAL.

We must not try to minister to people ON EMPTY. We must say NO TO SOME GOOD OPPORTUNITIES IN ORDER TO SAY YES TO GREAT OPPORTUNITIES TO RECEIVE FRESH POWER. Jesus told His disciples to WAIT AT JERUSALEM UNTIL THEY BE ENDUED WITH POWER FROM ON HIGH. **St Luke 24:49.** They continued with PRAYER AND SUPPLICATION FOR TEN DAYS. **Acts 1:14.** As a result, they led over 3000 people to Jesus.

We will accomplish much more if we get away from the crowd in order to get orders from our COMMANDER JESUS CHRIST.

Your Brother, Arthur Brown.

Sunday, January 09, 2019

Precious Saints, greetings

**Topic:** *Don't Allow Relaxing To Become Relapsing.*

**Text:** 1ˢᵗ Kings 13:11-14

"THE OLD PROPHET OF BETHEL FOUND THE MAN OF GOD SITTING UNDER AN OAK."

**Introduction:**

**Genesis 2; 2** says: "And on the seventh day God ended His work and rested." God established the Sabbath for man's benefit. He expects us to rest and relax. Jesus called His disciples to come aside and RELAX A WHILE. **Mark 6:31.** Many hardworking servants of God have suffered severe BURNOUT because they never took a break. Some even died PREMATURELY, because they were not wise enough.

However, today I wish to point out four of God's Servants who allowed RELAXING TO TURN INTO RELAPSING.

1. The young Prophet from Judah in **1ˢᵗ Kings 13** was RELAXING UNDER AN OAK TREE when the old Prophet from Bethel deceived him. This young Prophet was used mightily by God in Bethel, the hometown of the old prophet. He resisted the King's offer, yet while RELAXING UNDER A TREE, he succumbed to the deception of the old prophet. He died prematurely because of DISOBEDIENCE.

   Please don't allow your time of RELAXING TO BECOME A TIME OF RELAPSING.

2. Elijah, the mighty Man of God, was relaxing under a JUNIPER TREE when he uttered these words; "IT IS ENOUGH; NOW O LORD, TAKE AWAY MY LIFE; FOR I AM NOT BETTER THAN MY FATHERS." **1st Kings 19: 4** very soon after that, God sent him to appoint Elisha as his successor. **1st Kings 19: 15-21.**

3. The Prophet Jonah was exceedingly happy when God prepared A GOURD to shelter him from the sun. **Jonah 4: 6.** However, when God allowed a worm to destroy the tree, Jonah was upset with God. He uttered these words: "IT IS BETTER FOR ME TO DIE THAN TO LIVE." **Ch 4:8.** One would have thought that Jonah's experience in the belly of the fish would have humbled him. However, the book shows that he RELAPSED into a state of STUBBORNNESS.

4. Most persons will remember that David's time of RELAXING BECAME HIS WORST TIME OF RELAPSING. **2nd Samuel 11.** Just that he was RELAXING IN THE COMFORT OF HIS HOME and not under a tree.

**Conclusion:**

Moses spent 40 years in a secluded desert, but praise God; he never entered a state of RELAPSING. Joseph spent 13 years waiting on God to fulfill His promises. I'm happy that he never RELAPSED INTO SIN.

Please don't allow your time of RELAXING TO BECOME A TIME OF RELAPSING.

Your Brother, Arthur Brown.

Sunday, January 16, 2019

Precious Saints, greetings.

**Topic:** *MANY PREACHERS, BUT FEW FATHERS.*

**Text:** 1ˢᵗ Cor 4:15

"For though ye have, TEN THOUSAND INSTRUCTORS in Christ, yet have ye NOT MANY FATHERS, for in Christ Jesus I have begotten you through the Gospel."

**Introduction:**

Not many persons can genuinely call their Pastor "DADDY." Yet, people all over the world still refer to BISHOP SHAW AS DADDY SHAW. Preachers need to find the secrets for such AFFECTIONATE BONDING between members and Pastor.

I'm suggesting five of these secrets.

1.  Pastor must be a PRODUCER.

    Paul emphatically and proudly said: "I AM THE ONE WHO GAVE BIRTH TO YOU THROUGH CHRIST."

    Many pastors are only taking care of someone else's children. Preachers would be more AFFECTIONATE to their members if they were the ones who preached them out of sin.

2.  The Pastor must be a NURSING MOTHER.

    **1ˢᵗ Thessalonians 2:7** "BUT WE WERE GENTLE AMONG YOU, EVEN AS A NURSE CHERISHETH HER CHILDREN."

Breast milk is still the best for a young baby. It's very PATHETIC that many preachers have no milk to offer young believers.

At the time of feeding, the baby is getting both NUTRIENT AND CONTENTMENT.

Many members are suffering from MALNUTRITION because their pastor lacks the SINCERE MILK OF THE WORD OF GOD.

3.  The Pastor must be a WEEPER.

    In **Galatians 4:19,** Paul says: "MY LITTLE CHILDREN, OF WHOM I TRAVAIL IN BIRTH AGAIN UNTIL CHRIST BE FORMED IN YOU."

    Paul called his brethren MY LITTLE CHILDREN. More pastors need to use this terminology. He said I AM STILL CARRYING THE BIRTH PAIN. It won't cease until every believer is IMPREGNATED WITH CHRIST. We need more AGONIZING AND LESS ORGANIZING.

4.  The Pastor must be a REJOICER over the Believers' progress.

    **3rd John verse 4.** "I HAVE NO GREATER JOY THAN TO HEAR THAT MY CHILDREN WALK IN TRUTH."

    Preachers need to be far more expressive when they see their members are making progress. Most of us are programmed to CRITICIZE instead of COMPLIMENT. Children love when their parents articulate how proud they are of their progress. They need to hear Daddy say: "I AM EXTREMELY PROUD OF YOUR PROGRESS."

5.   The Pastor must be a REBUKER OF WRONGDOINGS.

   **Heb 12: 5-11**

   **Verse 9:** WE HAVE HAD FATHERS OF OUR FLESH WHICH CORRECTED US.

   We are called to DISCIPLINE OUR CHILDREN, not to PUNISH THEM. The best place to discipline them is IN A BATHTUB OF LOVE.

**Conclusion:**

On this FATHER'S Day, I am asking that fathers learn how to be AN AFFECTIONATE DAD.

1.   Be a PRODUCER OF CHILDREN.

2.   Be a NURSING MOTHER OF CHILDREN.

3.   Be a TRAILER FOR YOUR CHILDREN.

4.   Be a REJOICER OVER YOUR CHILDREN.

5.   Be a REBUKER OF YOUR CHILDREN'S WRONGDOINGS.

Happy FATHER'S DAY to our faithful and dedicated fathers.

Your Brother, Arthur Brown.

Sunday, January 30, 2019

Precious Saints, greetings.

**Topic:** *SAGACITY TURNS INTO STUPIDITY.*

**Text:** 1ˢᵗ Kings 11:9

"AND THE LORD WAS ANGRY WITH SOLOMON BECAUSE HIS HEART WAS TURNED FROM THE LORD GOD OF ISRAEL, WHICH APPEARED UNTO HIM TWICE."

**Introduction:**

The scripture explicitly states that God made Solomon WISER THAN ALL MEN. **1ˢᵗ Kings 4:31.** This SAGACIOUS SOLOMON BECAME A COLOSSAL FOOL.

He blatantly ignored God's FOUR RULES FOR A KING IN **DEUTERONOMY 17:16-17.**

1.  The King should not MULTIPLY HORSES

    **1ˢᵗ Kings 4:26** tells us that Solomon had forty thousand stalls of horses for his chariots and twelve thousand horsemen.

    His father, David, in **Psalm 20:7,** says:" SOME TRUST IN CHARIOTS AND SOME IN HORSES: BUT WE WILL REMEMBER THE NAME OF THE LORD OUR GOD."

    Solomon was SEEKING SECURITY.

2.  The King should not return to Egypt.

    King Solomon not only returned to Egypt, but he married Pharaoh's daughter and made her an elaborate palace. She turned his heart away from God. Abraham had made a similar mistake when he had a Son with an Egyptian girl. This mistake is plaguing the Jews until today.

Solomon was seeking POPULARITY.

3.  The King should not multiply wives to himself. Well, Solomon had a harem of 1000 pagan women who turned his heart away from the Lord.

    **Genesis 2:24** tells us that a man should cleave unto HIS WIFE.

    Paul states in **1ˢᵗ Timothy 3:2** THAT A BISHOP MUST BE THE HUSBAND OF ONE WIFE. We cannot ignore the word of God and get by.

    Solomon could not control his SEXUALITY. He was guilty of IMMORALITY.

4.  The King should not greatly multiply to himself SILVER AND GOLD.

    In **1ˢᵗ Kings 11:27**, we are told that Solomon made SILVER to be in Jerusalem like stones. He was so wealthy that he was able to import APES FOR FANCY AND PEACOCK FOR BEAUTY. **1ˢᵗ Kings 10:22.**

    He taxed his people heavily in order to maintain such elaborate lifestyle. Solomon's greatest downfall was HIS PROSPERITY.

**Conclusion:**

God told Solomon that He wasn't pleased with his behavior. Shortly after Solomon's death, the kingdom was divided. The kingdom that was characterized by PLENTY, LUXURY, AND PROSPERITY ENDED UP INTO CAPTIVITY.

Let's take God's word seriously. He is NO RESPECTER OF PERSON. He allowed even great King Solomon's SAGACITY TO TURN INTO STUPIDITY.

Let's avoid Solomon's mistakes.

Your Brother, Arthur Brown.


Sunday, March 30, 2019

Precious Saints.

Greetings.

**Topic:** *Our Deliverance Ministry Must Put The Devil's Businesses Into Bankruptcy.*

1.  The pig owners felt that their entire business was destroyed when Jesus, THE DELIVERANCE PREACHER CAME TO TOWN. **Mark 5.**

    It's very sad that some churches are putting on robes and rings on Prodigals while they are still in the hog pen. Some church members are ardent supporters of the devil's business.

2.  The masters of the girl with the spirit of divination were hopping mad when Paul DELIVERED THE DAMSEL.

    Our deliverance ministry will make some MAD, some SAD, and others GLAD.

The masters lost gain when Paul delivered the girl. Both Paul and Silas were thrown in prison. Let's remember, however, persecution cannot destroy the church. It will only cause the fire to spread faster.

3. When Paul, the deliverance preacher, arrived in Ephesus, the idol makers' business came under severe attack. **Acts 19.**

**Conclusion:**

An anemic church cannot be called DELIVERANCE CENTRE. We must get back our DISTINCTIVENESS. Our TRADEMARK HAS BEEN DELIVERANCE FOR ALL.

Therefore, let's put the devil out of business by driving out the demons and the hogs from our communities.

April 24, 2019

A Mark of Honor

**TODAY'S SCRIPTURE:**

"It is an honor for a man to cease from strife…."

Proverbs 20:3, AMP

**TODAY'S WORD:**

If we realized the destructive force that strife is, we would be more careful not to allow it into our relationships. It can creep into relationships by starting small, maybe through a comment or a wrong look from someone, and then escalate into something much bigger. When we let our guard down and say disrespectful, hurtful, or demeaning things, we're not just damaging our relationship; we're inviting the destructive spirit of strife into that relationship. But when you choose to cease from strife and overlook an offense, you are acting honorably and honoring God. How do you avoid strife? The Bible tells us that love covers over many offenses.

Love stops strife. It means that you give people the benefit of the doubt. You consider what they may be going through instead of focusing on how they reacted to you. Maybe someone was short with you at the office, but they may have a loved one in the hospital. Instead of getting upset, walk-in love—be patient and kind to them. Look for ways to walk in peace with the people in your life and put an end to strife!

**PRAYER FOR TODAY:**

"Father, thank You for Your hand of victory in my life. Give me the wisdom and courage I need to walk away from strife so that I can focus on the destiny You have prepared for me. I love You and bless You in Jesus' name. Amen."

Sunday, May 05, 2019

Precious Saints, greetings.

**Topic:** *Beware of the PARALYSIS OF PESSIMISM.*

**Text:** 1ˢᵗ Cor. 15:19 "IF IN THIS LIFE ONLY WE HAVE HOPE IN CHRIST, WE ARE ALL MEN MOST MISERABLE."

**Introduction:**

Our text clearly teaches that we should have HOPE IN CHRIST IN TWO LOCATIONS.

(1)  Earthbound hope
(2)  Heaven bound hope

1.   EARTHBOUND HOPE

In recent times, the quality of the hope of many Christians has ebbed away drastically. There is an unacknowledged and unexpressed fear in the hearts of many Christians that somehow the world has slipped beyond God's control. The early Christians had a bouncing optimism that we no longer possess. They had an indomitable hope that nothing could quench. The center of gravity of their hope was in the ETERNAL, not the temporal.

We must stride confidently despite the spirit of pessimism around us. REMEMBER, THE FUTURE IS AS BRIGHT AS THE PROMISES OF GOD. We must develop a sturdy and strong hope. We must divorce shallow optimism. Instead, we must cultivate and develop a steadfast and firm hope, which is fastened to Jesus, who is our anchor. We must continue to be the revolutionary light shining brightly in a very dark and dismal environment. One handful of salt can still heal the polluted water.

2.   Heaven bound Hope.

Paul In **Colossians 1:5** states, "THE HOPE WHICH IS LAID UP FOR YOU IN HEAVEN."

We believers must therefore be HEAVENLY MINDED. Jesus says: "WHERE YOUR TREASURE IS, THERE WILL YOUR HEART BE ALSO **Matt 6:21**

Jesus tells us that He is gone to prepare a place for us, and He is coming back for us. **St John 14:1-2.** The Apostle John writes: "BELOVED, NOW ARE WE THE SONS OF GOD, AND IT DOTH

NOT YET APPEAR WHAT WE SHALL BE, BUT WE KNOW THAT, WHEN HE SHALL APPEAR, WE SHALL BE LIKE HIM, FOR WE SHALL SEE HIM AS HE IS.

AND EVERY MAN THAT HATH THIS HOPE IN HIM PURIFIETH HIMSELF, EVEN AS HE IS PURE." **1st. John 3:2-3**

Our Heaven-bound hope will influence our character and behavior. This hope gives us a vivacious and buoyant spirit. We will continue to labor for the Lord, with the supreme knowledge, THAT THE BEST IS YET TO COME.

**Conclusion:**

The call to all of us is, GET RID OF LIMPING DOUBT AND REJOICE IN LEAPING FAITH.

Remember, faith is the substance of things HOPED FOR, the evidence of things not seen. **Heb 11:1** Don't be paralyzed by PESSIMISM, BUT RATHER ACTIVATE YOUR LIVELY HOPE.

Your Brother, Arthur Brown.

Sunday, May 12, 2019

Precious Saints, greetings.

**Topic:** *The Mother Who Loaned Her Son To God*

Permanently.

**Text:** 1ˢᵗ Sam 1:27-28.

"HANNAH SAID, "FOR THIS CHILD I PRAYED, AND THE LORD HATH GIVEN ME MY PETITION WHICH I ASKED OF HIM: THEREFORE ALSO I HAVE LENT HIM TO THE LORD, AS LONG AS HE LIVETH HE SHALL BE LENT TO THE LORD; AND HE WORSHIPPED THE LORD THERE."

**Introduction:**

Hannah demonstrates emphatically what mothers should do with their children. They should be given back to the Lord PERMANENTLY.

I have high admiration for Hannah for three reasons.

1.  SHE REMAINED FAITHFUL EVEN WHEN HER ADVERSARY DESPISED HUMILIATINGLY.

    Peninnah, Hannah's adversary, had sons and daughters, but Hannah was barren. **Ch1:6** says, "HER ADVERSARY PROVOKED HER SORE, TO MAKE HER FRET." But instead of retaliating and fretting, Hannah went in prayer and fasting. Dear MOTHERS, prayer and fasting are still two very effective weapons to destroy the attacks of your adversaries.

2. SHE REMAINED HUMBLE WHEN HER RELIGIOUS LEADER CRITICIZED HER WRONGFULLY.

Eli mistakenly accused Hannah of being drunk when she was sincerely making a request to God. **Ch1:15** Hannah said to Eli, NO MY LORD, I AM A WOMAN OF SORROWFUL SPIRIT, I HAVE DRUNK NEITHER WINE NOR STRONG DRINK, BUT HAVE POURED OUT MY SOUL BEFORE THE LORD.

Mothers, please maintain a meek and quiet spirit even in the midst of severe criticism. Rejoice and be exceedingly glad when you're wrongfully accused.

3. SHE GAVE BACK TO THE LORD GENEROUSLY WHEN HE REWARDED HER HANDSOMELY.

Samuel was the child Hannah desperately needed. Yet when the Lord blessed her bountifully, she gave him back unreservedly. Samuel became a very outstanding and well-loved PROPHET AND PRIEST in Israel. Eli's two sons died tragically. We hear nothing about Peninnah's children.

**Conclusion:**

To all mothers who have been serving the Lord faithfully, even though you are being despised humiliatingly and being criticized wrongfully, remember God is going to REWARD YOU HANDSOMELY.

This is so because you have loaned your children to the Lord PERMANENTLY.

Happy Mothers' Day.

Your Brother, Arthur Brown.

Sunday, May 19, 2019

Precious Saints, greetings

**Topic:** *IMMEDIATE OBEDIENCE DOESN'T GUARANTEE IMMEDIATE SUCCESS.*

**Text:** Exod: 5:22-23

And Moses returned unto the Lord, and said, Lord, wherefore hast thou so evil entreated this people? WHY IS IT THOU HAST SENT ME? For since I came to Pharaoh to speak in Thy name, he hath done evil to this people; NEITHER HAST THOU DELIVERED THY PEOPLE AT ALL.

**Introduction:**

The Scripture records that Moses hesitatingly obeyed God's call to go to Egypt. Please remember that Moses had previously attempted to be Israel's EMANCIPATOR, but his attempt proved abortive. His impulsive spirit had died down after forty years in the desert. When God sent him to Egypt, he reluctantly obeyed. However, our text tells us that instead of IMMEDIATE SUCCESS, he met OPPOSITION, DISAPPOINTMENT, AND DESPAIR.

Let's see three things that Moses encountered:

1.   MOSES ENCOUNTERED REJECTION:

(a) From Pharaoh.
Pharaoh disdainfully refused to let the people go. He added new rigors to the already overburdened slaves. He publicly laughed at Moses's request. He openly Rejected Moses.

(b) The Israelites rejected Moses.
The captains bitterly accused Moses for their additional burden. V21 THEY SAID UNTO MOSES AND AARON, THE LORD LOOK UPON YOU AND JUDGE YOU, BECAUSE YOU HAVE MADE OUR SAVOUR TO BE ABHORRED IN THE EYES OF PHARAOH."

They blamed Moses for what was happening to them.

2.  MOSES ENCOUNTERED A RETURN TO THE LORD.

Moses had to learn to RELY UPON THE LORD ALONE. Please remember that DELAY IS NOT DENIAL.

Immediate success many times leads to PRIDE. And PRIDE LEADS TO DESTRUCTION. We must all be aware of SELF- INFLATION. The arms of flesh will fall us. Let's all then RETURN TO THE LORD WHO SENDS US ON HIS MISSION. He alone will give us the directives.

3.  MOSES ENCOUNTERED RELIEF.

In ch 6:1, we find these comforting words: " THEN THE LORD SAID UNTO MOSES, 'NOW SHALT THOU SEE WHAT I WILL DO WITH PHARAOH: FOR WITH A STRONG HAND SHALL HE LET THEM GO AND WITH A STRONG HAND SHALL HE DRIVE THEM OUT OF THIS LAND, FOR I AM THE LORD. Please read **Ch 6:1-8** and see God great SEVEN I WILL.

**Conclusion:**

Seeming frustrations and setbacks don't necessarily mean that we're out of God's will; they may be great evidences that we're in His will. Those roadblocks are tests which God intends to use to bring greater blessings to us. Don't allow DELAYED SUCCESS TO

DISCOURAGE YOU. Please RETURN TO THE LORD, and HE WILL RELIEVE YOU OF YOUR DISAPPOINTMENT AND WILL REVIVE YOUR DESPAIRING SPIRIT.

Your Brother, Arthur Brown.


Sunday, October 01, 2019

Precious Saints greetings.

This is October, our annual MONTH OF PRAYER.

Our deliverance ministry has achieved much over the years because of the vision of Bishop Wilfred A Shaw. He faithfully obeyed God in establishing October as the Month of Prayer.

I'm happy that many continue to observe the pattern that was established many years ago. THE UNBROKEN PRAYER TRAIN.

God makes special mention of Daniel's 21 days of continuous prayer and fasting Dan 10:2-3

"IN THOSE DAYS I DANIEL WAS MOURNING THREE FULL WEEKS. I ATE NO PLEASANT BREAD, NEITHER CAME FLESH NOR WINE IN MY MOUTH, NEITHER DID I ANOINT MYSELF AT ALL, TILL THREE WHOLE WEEKS WERE FULFILLED."

Throughout the scriptures, most of God's Servants spent quality time in prayer and fasting.

Jesus Himself launched His Ministry with 40 days of fasting and prayer. On many occasions, He spent the ENTIRE NIGHT IN PRAYER.

**Acts 12:5** says: "PETER THEREFORE WAS KEPT IN PRISON: BUT PRAYER WAS MADE WITHOUT CEASING OF THE CHURCH UNTO GOD FOR HIM."

**1ˢᵗ Thes 5:17** says: PRAY WITHOUT CEASING."

**Acts 4:31** tells us about PRAYER THAT SHOOK BUILDING. Please remember that Paul and Silas were worshipping AT MIDNIGHT WHEN THEIR WORSHIP SHOOK THE PRISON DOORS. **Act 16:25-26.**

I'm therefore encouraging us to engage in meaningful prayer vigils during this MONTH OF PRAYER.

Please include the entire congregation in this activity on Sundays also. We are going to see astronomical results because of the prayers of the Saints.

Elijah's prayer brought down fire from heaven. James 5:17 says he was a man just like us. THE EFFECTUAL PRAYER OF A RIGHTEOUS MAN AVAILETH MUCH **v 16.**

I'm confident that we're going to see growth and expansion after our MONTH OF PRAYER.

May God help us to remember that PRAYERLESSNESS LEADS TO DIZZINESS.

Your Brother, Arthur Brown.

Wednesday, October 02, 2019

Precious Saints, greetings,

**Topic:** *A BLESSING FOR THE EARLY RISERS.*

**Text:** St Mark 1:35

AND IN THE MORNING, RISING UP A GREAT WHILE BEFORE DAY, HE WENT OUT, AND DEPARTED INTO A SOLITARY PLACE, AND THERE PRAYED.

Jesus knew the secrets and benefits of RISING EARLY IN THE MORNING.

1.  The FRESHNESS OF THE AIR.

    No air pollution. You're able to breathe clean oxygen. Just go out early and breathe in Jesus. In HIM WE LIVE, AND MOVE, AND HAVE OUR BEING. **Acts 17:28**

2.  THE STILLNESS AND CALMNESS OF THE ENVIRONMENT.

    No noise pollution.

    "BE STILL AND KNOW THAT I AM GOD." **Psalm 46:10.** Let's recapture the FINE ART OF MEDITATION.

3.  THE GLORIOUSNESS OF THE ENVIRONMENT.

    "THE HEAVENS DECLARE THE GLORY OF GOD: AND THE FIRMAMENT SHEWETH HIS HANDIWORK." **Psalm 19:1**

Most of us are missing out on the greatest revelation of God because we refuse to go out early in the morning and see the majestic glory of God in His creation.

During this month of PRAYER, choose some outdoor locations.

Eg: Paul attended a PRAYER MEETING AT A RIVERSIDE. **Acts 16:13.**

Jesus went up into the mountains on many occasions to PRAY.

Jesus went into a garden to PRAY. He enjoyed the seaside for His prayer time also.

Please don't do all the praying indoor. And remember: EARLY BIRD CATCHES THE MOST WORMS.

Your Brother, Arthur Brown.


Sunday, August 30, 2020

Precious saints greetings.

**Topic:** *FLEE FROM SOMETHINGS DESPERATELY, FOLLOW SOMETHINGS DETERMINEDLY, FIGHT FOR SOMETHINGS DOGGEDLY.*

**Text:** 1st Timothy 6:11 -12.

"But thou, O man of God, FLEE, these things; and FOLLOW after righteousness, godliness, faith, love, patience, meekness.

FIGHT the good fight of faith.

## INTRODUCTION:

Paul placed Timothy in the company of some STALWARTS SAINTS when he called him MAN OF GOD. This name was given to:

(a)  Moses **Deuteronomy 33:1**
(b)  Samuel **1ˢᵗ Sam 9:6**
(c)  Elijah **1ˢᵗ Kings 17:18**
(d)  David **Nehemiah 12: 24.**

Paul encouraged Timothy to do three things.

1.  FLEE FROM SOME THINGS DESPERATELY.

    There are times when FLEEING is a mark of cowardice.

    Nehemiah said: "SHOULD SUCH A MAN AS I FLEE?" **Neh 6:11**

    There are times when FLEEING is a mark of wisdom. Joseph FLED from TEMPTATIONS. **Gen 39: 12.** David FLED when Saul tried to kill him. **1ˢᵗ Samuel 19:10.**

    The admonition Paul gives in our text is for the believers to SEPARATE themselves from UNGODLINESS.

    Paul wants us to know that not all UNITY is good, and not all DIVISIONS are bad.

    In **2ⁿᵈ Corinthians 6:17,** he says, "COME OUT FROM AMONG THEM AND BE YE SEPARATE."

    In **1ˢᵗ Corinthians 6: 8,** Paul tells us to FLEE FORNICATION.

    The best way to resist the devil is to FLEE FROM HIS TRAPS.

2. FOLLOW SOME THINGS DETERMINEDLY.

Separation without positive growth becomes ISOLATION. Therefore, we must become hardworking farmers and cultivate the following FRUIT.

(a) RIGHTEOUSNESS
This speaks of our personal integrity and character.

(b) GODLINESS
This speaks of our practical conduct and practices.

(c) FAITH OR FAITHFULNESS.
The believers must possess a high level of DEPENDABILITY.

(d) LOVE.
This is agape love which seeks to give and not to gain.

(e) PATIENCE
This is having the ability to have endurance during tough situations.

(f) MEEKNESS
This is not talking about weakness but GENTLENESS.

**2ⁿᵈ Corinthians 10: 1** tells us that Jesus has both MEEKNESS AND GENTLENESS. We must demonstrate that we have the ability to put POWER UNDER CONTROL.

3. FIGHT SOME THINGS DOGGEDLY.

Paul testified that he had FOUGHT A GOOD FIGHT. **2ⁿᵈ Tim 4;7.**

**Nehemiah 4:17** teaches that we must use the TROWEL FOR BUILDING AND THE SWORD FOR BATTLING.

In **2<sup>nd</sup> Corinthians 10: 4- 6,** Paul tells us to use our mighty WEAPONS to CAST DOWN imaginations

To bring into CAPTIVITY every thought to the obedience of Christ.

To REVENGE all DISOBEDIENCE.

## CONCLUSION:

Paul gives strong warning that believers: should FLEE from harmful lusts which drown men in destruction and perdition. **Ch 6: 9**

Riches are a trap which leads to bondage, not freedom. Wealth lacks both SECURITY AND DURABILITY.

The believers must be strong, tenacious FOLLOWERS of good lifestyles and practices. They must become active FIGHTERS against evil desires and practices—excellent advice for CHRISTIAN SOLDIERS.

Your Brother, Arthur Brown.


Sunday, September 20, 2020

Precious saints' greetings.

Topic: THE BELIEVER'S THREE TYPES OF WASHINGS.

**Text:** Ephesians 5:25-27

"Husbands love your wives, even as Christ also loves the church, and gave Himself for it; that He might sanctify and cleanse it with the WASHING OF WATER BY THE WORD, that He might present it to Himself a glorious church, not having spot, or wrinkle, or any such thing; but that it should be holy and without blemish."

## INTRODUCTION:

Our text tells us that Christ desires that every believer be cleansed, be spotless, be without wrinkles and blemishes.

Three times in scriptures, we find that there must be SPECIAL WASHING.

1. THERE MUST BE THE SOVEREIGN WASHING OF GOD.

    **Psalm 51:7** says: "Purge me with hyssop, and I shall be clean, wash me, and I shall be whiter than snow."

    At the first Passover in Egypt, HYSSOP was used to apply the blood to the door post. **Exodus 12:22.**

    **John 1:7** tells us: "THE BLOOD OF JESUS CHRIST HIS SON CLEANSETH US FROM ALL SIN."

    In **Hebrews 9:14,** we are told that: "THE BLOOD OF CHRIST PURGE OUR CONSCIENCE FROM DEAD WORK TO SERVE THE LIVING GOD."

    verse 22 states, "WITHOUT THE SHEDDING OF BLOOD IS NO REMISSION." And Hebrews 10:10 states that: "WE ARE SANCTIFIED THROUGH THE OFFERING OF THE BODY OF JESUS CHRIST, ONCE FOR ALL."

2. THE BELIEVER'S RESPONSIBILITY TO TAKE DAILY BATHS.

    **ISAIAH 1:16** says

    WASH you, make you clean, put away the evil of your doings from before Mine eyes, cease to do evil."

According to Paul in **Ephesians 5:26,** the believers must CONSTANTLY AND CONSISTENTLY bathe themselves in the WORD OF GOD. Jesus says in **St John 15:3,** "YE ARE CLEAN THROUGH THE WORD."

**St John 17:17,** Jesus prayed: "SANCTIFY THEM THROUGH THY TRUTH, THY WORD IS TRUTH."

**PSALM 119:9** tells us that a person is cleansed by TAKING HEED TO THE WORD OF GOD.

In **Esther 2: 12,** Esther spent TWELVE MONTHS in PURIFICATION AND BEAUTIFICATION before she appeared before the king.

Paul tells the believers in **2$^{nd}$ Corinthians 7:1,** "LET US CLEANSE OURSELVES FROM ALL FILTHINESS OF THE FLESH AND SPIRIT, PERFECTING HOLINESS IN THE FEAR OF GOD."

According to James, we should use the word AS MIRROR to discover our fault, but we should use the word AS WATER to remove the dirt. **James 1:23-25.**

Paul EMPHATICALLY tells us in **1$^{st}$ Timothy 5:22**

"KEEP THYSELF PURE."

3.  THE BELIEVER'S RESPONSIBILITY TO WASH ONE ANOTHER'S FEET.

Jesus in **St John 13:14** says: "YE OUGHT TO WASH ONE ANOTHER'S FEET."

According to Romans 3:23, ALL HAVE SINNED AND COME SHORT OF THE GLORY OF GOD.

Verse 10 says: THERE IS NONE RIGHTEOUS, NO NOT ONE.

Jesus told those without SIN to stone the woman in **St John 8:7.**

Paul in **Galatians 6:1** says that as believers, we have a ministry of RESTORATION.

Jesus told the parable of THE GOOD SAMARITAN in **Luke 10: 30-37** to teach us our responsibility to clean the wounds of others who have been beaten up by satan; he is a thief and robber.

Let us be like the dogs that compassionately LICKED LAZARUS' SORES. Let's not bite and devour one another.

Let's get water and towel and clean up the UGLINESS of our brethren.

## CONCLUSION:

We must note

1.  ONLY GOD CAN WASH AWAY OUR SIN, permanently using the blood of Jesus Christ.

2.  We must CONSTANTLY AND DAILY USE THE WORD OF GOD TO WASH AWAY ALL FILTHINESS OF THE FLESH AND THE spirit.

3.  WE MUST USE LOVE TO COMPASSIONATELY WASH ONE ANOTHER'S DIRTY FEET.

Since God has WASHED US, we ought to WASH ourselves and others also.

Your Brother, Arthur Brown.

Sunday, October 18, 2020

**Topic:** THE INFLEXIBILITY OF GOD'S ENTRY REQUIREMENTS INTO HIS PRIESTHOOD.

**TEXT:** Leviticus 8: 6-14

"And Moses brought Aaron and sons, and washed them with water, he clothed him with robe, he put the mitre upon his head, he poured the anointing oil upon Aaron's head and sanctify him, and they laid their hands upon the head of the ram of consecration."

## INTRODUCTION:

According to **1ˢᵗ Peter 2:9,** every believer belongs to God's ROYAL PRIESTHOOD. Also, twice in Revelation, we are told that BELIEVERS ARE MADE KINGS AND PRIESTS. **Ch 1: 6** and **Ch 5: 10.**

Our text gives us FIVE INFLEXIBLE REQUIREMENTS for those who are given a high calling to God's priesthood.

1. HE MUST BE THOROUGHLY CLEANSED. Verse 6 "Moses brought Aaron and his sons and WASHED THEM WITH WATER" According to **1ˢᵗ John 1: 7,** "THE BLOOD OF JESUS CHRIST, CLEANSETH US FROM ALL SIN" Paul in **Titus 3: 5** says that we are saved by THE WASHING OF REGENERATION AND RENEWING OF THE HOLY GHOST.

2. HE MUST BE BEAUTIFULLY CLOTHED. VERSE 7 "And Moses put upon him the coat, girded him with the girdle, and clothed him with the robe." In **Zechariah ch 3,** God took away the filthy garment that Joshua the High Priest had on, and replaced them with new priestly ROBE. We are now clothed in THE RIGHTEOUSNESS

OF JESUS CHRIST. **ISAIAH 64:6** says: ALL OUR RIGHTEOUSNESS ARE AS FILTHY RAGS.

3. HE MUST BE ROYALLY CROWNED. verse 9 "And Moses put MITRE upon his head." **Leviticus 21:12** calls it the CROWN OF ANOINTING. This crown represents the HELMET OF SALVATION. His mind is secured from the infiltration of evil thoughts. According to **Exodus 28:36-37,** these words must be written on the crown: HOLINESS TO THE LORD.

4. HE MUST BE TOTALLY CLAIMED. **Verse 12** "And he poured the anointing oil upon Aaron's head, and anointed him to SANCTIFY HIM. This speaks both of his sanctification and the anointing of the Holy Ghost. In **Luke 4:18,** Jesus says: THE SPIRIT OF THE LORD IS UPON ME. He is now totally controlled by the Holy Ghost.

5. HE MUST BE SACRIFICIALLY CONSECRATED. **Verse 22** "And Moses brought the RAM OF CONSECRATION AND AARON AND HIS SONS LAID THEIR HANDS UPON THE HEAD OF THE RAM. The animal acted as a SUBSTITUTE for the priests. When the animal died, THEY DIED. Their sins were transferred to the animal. Of course, this animal REPRESENTS JESUS, THE LAMB OF GOD WHO TAKES AWAY THE SIN OF THE WORLD. We must also note that Moses put blood upon their RIGHT EARS. They must always hear from God. Blood was placed upon the thumbs of the right hands. They must fearlessly execute their responsibilities; Blood was placed upon the big toes of their right feet. They had the authority to trample demons. Blood was poured out around the altar. The ALTAR REPRESENTS THE CROSS. This is a place of crucifixion.

## CONCLUSION:

It is unfortunate that many Christians don't read Leviticus. One wonders if it is because of the frequency of the word HOLY, which appears over 100 times. I feel strongly that many persons are scared of the harsh penalties that were given for disobedience. For example, God killed two of Aaron's sons who were just inducted into the PRIESTHOOD. They offered STRANGE FIRE. **Leviticus ch 10.**

In **Mal 3: 6,** we read, I AM THE LORD, I CHANGE NOT. And **Heb 12: 29** says: GOD IS A CONSUMING FIRE. Verse 28 says, "WHEREFORE WE RECEIVING A KINGDOM WHICH CANNOT BE MOVED, LET US HAVE GRACE, WHEREBY WE MAY SERVE GOD ACCEPTABLY WITH REVERENCE AND GODLY FEAR. Let's always remember that His requirements are INFLEXIBLE.

Your Brother, Arthur Brown.

**TEXT:** James 1:27 "PURE RELIGION AND UNDEFILED BEFORE GOD AND THE FATHER IS THIS, TO VISIT THE FATHERLESS AND THE WIDOWS IN THEIR AFFLICTION, AND TO KEEP HIMSELF UNSPOTTED FROM THE WORLD.

## INTRODUCTION:

The world is a very filthy place. **1ˢᵗ John 2: 16** says: "ALL THAT'S IN THE WORLD are:

(a) lust of the flesh
(b) lust of the eyes
(c) the pride of life.

Jesus was a LAMB WITHOUT BLEMISH AND SPOT. The Apostle Jude tells us that Jesus wants to present us FAULTLESS WITH EXCEEDING JOY. **Verse 24.**

Paul in **Ephesians 5:26-27** says it is Jesus' desire to present His church as A BRIDE, not having spots or wrinkles, but holy and without blemishes.

Let's divide today's meditation into two parts:

**FIRSTLY:** THE NECESSITY OF UNSPOTTEDNESS

**Isaiah 52:11** says: "BE YE CLEAN THAT BEAR THE VESSEL OF THE LORD." **Isaiah,** in chapter 6, says God had to cleanse him before He could use him.

According to **Matthew 5: 8,** ONLY THOSE WHO ARE PURE IN HEART can fellowship with God. **Habakkuk 1:13** says: "GOD IS TOO PURE TO BEHOLD EVIL AND TO LOOK ON INIQUITY."

IN **2ⁿᵈ Corinthians 7: 1,** Paul commands the believers, "TO CLEANSE THEMSELVES FROM ALL FILTHINESS OF THE FLESH AND SPIRIT."

David tells us in **1ˢᵗ Chronicles 29:17** that God HATH PLEASURE IN UPRIGHTNESS.

In **1ˢᵗ Corinthians 6: 9-10,** Paul gives a long list of uncleanliness that cannot be tolerated in the Kingdom of God. He told the brethren that they are WASHED AND SANCTIFIED BY JESUS AND THE HOLY SPIRIT.

**SECONDLY:** THE REMEDY FOR SPOTTEDNESS

(A) According to **1ˢᵗ John 1:7,** "The BLOOD OF JESUS CHRIST cleanseth us from all sin.

John in **Rev 1: 5** tells us that because Jesus loves us, He uses His BLOOD TO WASH US FROM SIN.

**Hebrews 9: 13 -14** says: "If the BLOOD of bulls and of goats and the ashes of an heifer sprinkling the unclean, sanctifieth to the purging of the flesh, HOW MUCH MORE SHALL THE BLOOD OF CHRIST, who through eternal Spirit offered Himself without spot to God, PURGE your conscience from dead works to serve the living God. **Verse 22** says WITHOUT THE SHEDDING OF BLOOD IS NO REMISSION.

(B) The word of God, which is comparable to water, is also a CLEANSING AGENT.

In **Ephesians 5: 26,** Paul tells us that Jesus cleanses His church WITH THE WASHING OF WATER BY THE WORD.

In **St John 15:3,** Jesus says, WE ARE CLEAN THROUGH THE WORDS WHICH HE HAS SPOKEN.

In **John 17:17,** He asked His Father to SANCTIFY HIS FOLLOWERS BY THE WORD OF TRUTH.

**Psalm 119:9** says, IT IS ONLY THE WORD OF GOD THAT CAN CLEANSE AND KEEP A YOUNG MAN CLEAN.

At the Tabernacle, immediately after the BLOODY BRAZEN ALTAR, the priests went TO THE LAVER TO WASH before they entered THE HOLY PLACE.

(C) THE FIRE OF THE HOLY GHOST IS THE OTHER CLEANSING AGENT.

In **Matthew 3:11-12,** John The Baptist emphatically states that Jesus will baptize HIS FOLLOWERS WITH THE HOLY GHOST AND WITH FIRE, and this FIRE SHALL PURGE THE FLOOR, BURN UP CHAFF.

**Hebrews 12:29** states: "GOD IS A CONSUMING FIRE."

At the burning bush in **Exodus 3**, MOSES WAS TOLD TO REMOVE HIS FILTHY SHOES. Moses told the priests in **Leviticus 6:3,** "ENSURE THAT FIRE IS CONTINUOUSLY ON THE ALTAR."

## CONCLUSION:

According to **2nd Kings 5:14,** when Naaman dipped seven times in Jordan, his flesh came again like unto the flesh of a little child.

Paul in **2nd Timothy 2:20-21** tells us that in a great house, there are various types of vessels, however for them to be USEFUL, THEY MUST BE PURGED, SANCTIFIED AND BE PREPARED FOR GOOD WORK.

In **2nd Peter 2: 21-22,** we are warned that turning away from the way of righteousness is like: A DOG TURNING TO ITS OWN VOMIT, OR AS A SOW THAT WAS WASHED TO HER WALLOWING IN THE MIRE.

**HEBREWS 10:22** puts it beautifully: "LET US DRAW NEAR WITH A TRUE HEART IN FULL ASSURANCE OF FAITH, HAVING OUR HEARTS SPRINKLED FROM EVIL CONSCIENCE AND OUR BODIES WASHED WITH PURE WATER."

Saints, let's obey Paul's command:

"KEEP THYSELF PURE." **1ˢᵗ Timothy 5:22.**

Your Brother, Arthur Brown.


Sunday, November 01, 2020

**Topic:** *Departure From Sin Is Demanded*

*Text:* **2ⁿᵈ Timothy 2:19**

"LET EVERY ONE THAT NAMETH THE NAME OF CHRIST DEPART FROM INIQUITY."

**INTRODUCTION:**

Christian belief and behavior MUST be intricately intertwined. It is inevitable that God's children practice righteousness. There is an alarming and frightening level of indiscipline that is prevailing in many churches today. Many people have developed a craving appetite for UNGODLINESS. Pastors cannot afford to turn a blind eye to the level of REBELLIOUSNESS that has invaded our churches. We must remember that one TOXIC BELIEVER can defile an entire church. Paul in **1ˢᵗ. Corinthians 5: 7-8** begs that we PURGE OUT THE OLD LEAVEN THAT CAN EASILY CONTAMINATE THE ENTIRE DOUGH. In scripture, LEAVEN is a symbol for SIN.

In this meditation, let us examine FIVE TYPES OF LEAVEN.

    A.  THE LEAVEN OF MALICE AND WICKEDNESS.

        **1ˢᵗ Corinthians 5:8 says:** "Let us keep the feast, NOT with the old leaven, neither with the LEAVEN OF MALICE

AND WICKEDNESS; but with the UNLEAVENED BREAD OF SINCERITY AND TRUTH." In **Ephesians 4:31,** Paul admonishes us: "LET ALL BITTERNESS, AND WRATH AND ANGER AND CLAMOUR AND EVIL SPEAKING, BE PUT AWAY FROM YOU WITH ALL MALICE. **Hebrews 12:15** tells us that many believers have allowed the root of BITTERNESS to spring up in their hearts and caused DEFILEMENT. Jesus in **Matthew 18: 34** clearly states that those with unforgiving spirit are turned over to the TORMENTORS.

B.   THE LEAVEN OF HYPOCRISY

In **Luke 12: 1,** Jesus says that the Pharisees were the main culprits of this LEAVEN. In **Matthew 23,** EIGHT times, Jesus says: "WOE UNTO THE PHARISEES." Jesus denounces HYPOCRISY vehemently. The harshest and most stinging denouncement was when Jesus likened their HYPOCRISY to the whited sepulcher. Outwardly they appeared beautiful, but inwardly they were full of rottenness. God hates PRETENSE but loves GENUINENESS.

David set an excellent example when he acknowledged his sins REPENTANTLY and asked for forgiveness SINCERELY.

C.   THE LEAVEN OF PRIDE AND WORLDLINESS.

**Mark 8: 15** says: "BEWARE OF THE LEAVEN OF HEROD."

We must remember that Herod took away his brother's wife and killed John The Baptist when he rebuked him.

But hear these words, which are recorded in **Acts 12:21-23.**

"And upon a set day, HEROD arrayed himself in royal apparel, sat upon his throne, and made an oration unto them. And the people gave a shout, saying

"IT IS THE VOICE OF A god, NOT OF A MAN."

And immediately the angel of the Lord smote him, because he gave NOT GOD THE GLORY: and he was eaten of worms and gave up the ghost."

**1ˢᵗ Corinthians 1: 29** remind us, "NO FLESH SHOULD GLORY IN GOD'S PRESENCE."

D.  THE LEAVEN OF UNBELIEF.

In **Matthew 16: 6,** Jesus says: BEWARE OF THE LEAVEN OF THE SADDUCEES. In **Matthew 22:23** and **Acts 23:8,** we are told that the Sadducees say that THERE ARE NO RESURRECTION, NEITHER ANGELS NOR SPIRITS.

We know that these are the bedrock and fundamental doctrines upon which Christianity is built. Deviation from foundational TRUTHS always leads to loose BEHAVIOUR.

E.  THE LEAVEN OF FALSE DOCTRINE.

In **Galatians 5:9,** Paul says it only takes a minute amount of yeast to permeate an entire dough. Paul was correcting the false doctrine of SALVATION BY LAW that the brethren were reverting to. The yeast of false doctrine can be quickly, quietly, and subtly introduced in a church. We must COURAGEOUSLY keep false doctrines out of our churches.

## Conclusion:

The Holy Ghost dealt ruthlessly and brutally with Ananias and Sapphira, because their unscrupulous behavior was about to DESTROY THE INFANT CHURCH. We have been QUENCHING the HOLY GHOST in our churches because we are afraid HE MAY GET RID OF SOME OF OUR STRONG FINANCIAL SUPPORTERS.

Let's preach righteousness THUNDEROUSLY less the HOLY GHOST depart from our churches COMPLETELY.

Your, Brother Arthur Brown.


Sunday, November 15, 2020

Precious Saints Greetings

**Topic:** No Challenge, No Growth

**Text:** Jeremiah 12: 5

"If thou hast run with the footmen, and they have wearied thee, then how canst thou contend with horses? and if in the land of peace, wherein thou trustedst, they wearied thee, then how wilt thou do in the swelling of Jordan?"

## Introduction:

Easy life stifles maturity; difficult life challenges us to develop our spiritual muscles. God never promised Jeremiah an easy job, but He promised him all the equipment to do the job faithfully. Let's learn THREE great lessons from our text.

A.  THE LIFE OF GODLY SERVICE IS NOT EASY.

This life is like running a RACE. God asked Jeremiah some serious questions: "IF YOU FIND IT DIFFICULT TO KEEP UP WITH FOOTMEN, HOW ARE YOU GOING TO KEEP UP WITH HORSES?" In **Phil 3:14,** Paul tells us that this race requires STRENUOUS PRESSING.

Booker T Washington, the great black American, said, "YOU MEASURE THE SIZE OF THE ACCOMPLISHMENT BY THE OBSTACLES YOU HAVE TO OVERCOME TO REACH YOUR GOALS. "We must give ourselves a strong dose of VACCINE against comfort and complacency. A great one-handed golfer said, "The right attitude and one arm will beat the wrong attitude and two arms every time."

B.  THE LIFE OF GODLY SERVICE GETS HARDER, NOT EASIER.

Notice that our text says Jeremiah started out with FOOT SOLDIERS, then the intensity of the race increased to HORSES, THEN TO THE SWELLING OF JORDAN RIVER. As the race progressed, the difficulty of the obstacles increased.

Most of us have used WD 40 to loosen a tight screw or bolt but don't know what it stands for or the story behind it. IT MEANS WATER DISPLACEMENT 40th ATTEMPT. In 1953 Rocket Chemical Company set out to create a rust-prevention solvent. It took them 40 attempts to perfect the formula. Like the people in this company, we must push through the dark corridors of difficulty in order to achieve our goals. ENDURANCE AND PERSEVERANCE MUST BE OUR ROD AND STAFF IN THIS VERY CHALLENGING RACE.

## C. THE LIFE OF GODLY SERVICE GETS BETTER AS WE GROW MORE MATURE.

Jeremiah's life never got easier; however, he handled all the challenges in an admirable way. He faced several imprisonments, ridicules, death threats, his scrolls burned by the King. They called him a traitor, yet his ministry lasted approximately forty-six years. God built his character in the furnace of affliction. He came out as pure gold. His life was characterized by longevity and tenacity.

In 1914 when Thomas Edison's great laboratories were destroyed by fire in New Jersey, he lost two million dollars. The sixty-seven-year-old said, "THERE IS GREAT VALUE IN DISASTER; ALL OUR MISTAKES ARE BURNED UP. THANK GOD! WE CAN START ALL OVER AGAIN."

**Conclusion:**

John Wesley was walking with a friend who was defeated by problems that were facing him. During their walk, they saw a cow looking over a stone wall. "Do you know why that cow is looking over that stone wall? "asked Wesley, "No," replied the friend. "Because she can't see through it," Wesley said. "And that is what you must do with all your wall of trouble, look over it and avoid it."

At age 85 years, Caleb asked for the mountainous area where the giants lived. Nothing could stop him from claiming his inheritance. The process of education is full of challenging examinations. A truly educated person must exhibit signs of CHANGES AND GROWTH.

Here's a three-fold formula for SPIRITUAL GROWTH:

1. GET INTO THE RACE AND STAY IN IT.
2. ACCEPT THE CHALLENGES OF THE RACE.
3. MAKE PROGRESSIVE STRIDES, AND FINISH THE RACE.

Your Brother, Arthur Brown.


Sunday, November 22, 2020

Precious Saints Greetings.

**Topic:** AN URGENT NEED FOR A MASSIVE PRAISE PROGRAMME.

**Text:** Psalm 150: 6

"LET EVERYTHING THAT HATH BREATH PRAISE THE LORD. PRAISE YE THE LORD."

**Introduction:**

There must be perpetual, purposeful, and aggressive praise in the church. Praise is the fire that must constantly burn on the altar. Praise is the spark plug that ignites the engine of the church. It is the detergent that purifies and purges doubts from the church. Triumphant and continuous praise must be a way of life for the church. Let's examine FIVE EXAMPLES when massive praise programs were organized.

A. AFTER THE CROSSING OF THE RED SEA, MIRIAM THE PROPHETESS ORGANIZED A MASSIVE PRAISE PROGRAMME. **Exodus 15: 20-21.**

"Miriam took a timbrel, and ALL the women went out after her with timbres and with dances. And Miriam answered them, "SING YE TO THE LORD, FOR HE HATH TRIUMPHED GLORIOUSLY; THE HORSE AND HIS RIDER HATH HE THROWN INTO THE SEA.""

B. WHEN DAVID BROUGHT THE ARK TO JERUSALEM, HE ORGANIZED A MASSIVE PRAISE PROGRAMME. **2ⁿᵈ Samuels 6:1-15.**

Verse 5 "DAVID AND ALL THE HOUSE OF ISRAEL PLAYED BEFORE THE LORD ON ALL MANNER OF INSTRUMENTS MADE OF FIR WOOD, EVEN ON HARPS, AND PSALTERIES, AND ON TIMBRELS, AND CORNETS, AND ON CYMBALS."

C. WHEN SOLOMON DEDICATED THE TEMPLE THE ALTAR WAS TOO SMALL TO RECEIVE ALL THE SACRIFICES. THE CELEBRATION OF PRAISE LASTED 14 DAYS. **1ˢᵗ. Kings 8: 64-66.**

Verse 65 "And at that time Solomon held a feast, and ALL Israel with him, a great congregation, from the entering in Hamath unto the river of Egypt, before the Lord our God seven days and seven days, even fourteen days."

D. WHEN ZERUBBABEL LAID THE FOUNDATION OF THE POST-EXILIC TEMPLE, THERE WAS A MASSIVE PRAISE SERVICE. **EZRA 3:10-11.**

"When the builders laid the foundation of the Temple of the Lord, they set the priests in their apparel with trumpets, and the Levites the sons of Asaph with cymbals, TO PRAISE THE LORD, after the ordinance of David king of Israel. And they sang together by course in PRAISING AND GIVING THANKS UNTO THE LORD."

E. WHEN NEHEMIAH COMPLETED THE REBUILDING OF THE WALL IN JUST FIFTY TWO DAYS, HE ORGANIZED A CHOIR OF 245 members to do a massive PRAISE PROGRAMME. **Nehemiah 7:67.**

**Conclusion:**

Perhaps the greatest PRAISE PROGRAMME in the Bible was organized by King Jehoshaphat in **2ⁿᵈ Chronicles 20**. The nation was under attack by Ammon, Moab and Mount Seir. The Holy Spirit revealed that they should not be afraid, but expressly said: "THE BATTLE IS NOT YOURS, BUT GOD'S." "YE NEED NOT FIGHT IN THIS BATTLE."

Verse 19 "THE LEVITES STOOD UP TO PRAISE THE LORD GOD OF ISRAEL WITH A LOUD VOICE ON HIGH.

PLEASE READ VERSE 22 for yourself.

"AND WHEN THEY BEGAN TO SING AND TO PRAISE, THE LORD SET AMBUSHMENTS AGAINST THE CHILDREN OF AMMON, MOAB, AND MOUNT SEIR, WHICH WERE COME AGAINST JUDAH; AND THEY WERE SMITTEN."

It is indeed amazing what PRAISES can do. In a period when Satan's desire is the neutralize the church, my earnest cry is for the church TO TURN UP OUR PRAISE VOLUME. Let's deafen all the negativity that is trying to SILENCE THE CHURCH.

Hence an urgent need for A MASSIVE PRAISE PROGRAMME in all of God's churches.

Your Brother, Arthur Brown.

Sunday, November 29, 2020

Precious Saints Greetings.

**Topic:** Be Tender with Sinners, But Be Tough with Sin.

**Text:** Jude 22-23

"AND OF SOME HAVE COMPASSION, MAKING A DIFFERENCE: AND OTHERS SAVED WITH FEAR, PULLING THEM OUT OF THE FIRE; HATING EVEN THE GARMENT SPOTTED BY THE FLESH."

**Introduction:**

Our text tells us that we are to COMPASSIONATELY rescue sinners, but we are to hate sin PASSIONATELY. The book of Jude is one of the neglected books of the Bible. It is overshadowed by lofty Revelation, and because of its strong message, we don't read it much. I am imploring everyone to study this minor book, only 25 verses, that has a MAJOR MESSAGE FOR OUR TIME.

**THE MESSAGE OF JUDE IS:**

"FIGHT WITH EVERYTHING YOU HAVE IN YOU, FOR THE FAITH WHICH WAS ENTRUSTED TO YOU. GUARD AND CHERISH IT PASSIONATELY. People were infiltrating the young church with serious and dangerous errors. Their design was to replace THE STRONG GOSPEL OF JESUS CHRIST WITH SOFT IMITATION.

Jude clearly shows how God disciplined those who defected from THE WAY OF TRUTH. He warns that we must beware of:

1. The way of Cain
2. The error of Balaam
3. The gainsaying of Korah

We are asked to remember what God did to Sodom and the rebellious angels that were cast out of heaven. The book is really warning us to be careful of the epidemic of wandering away from the PATH OF RIGHTEOUSNESS. Jude is telling us that when DEADLY VIRUS attacks the church, we must not be casual with it like how the Americans respond to COVID-19. There must be an energetic watchfulness for any deviation from the PATH OF RIGHTEOUSNESS.

Listen to how Jude describes the way of the UNGODLY in verses 22-23 in Eugene Peterson's

**Message:**

"THESE PEOPLE ARE WARTS ON YOUR LOVE FEASTS AS YOU EAT AND WORSHIP TOGETHER.

THEY'RE GIVING YOU BLACK EYE CAROUSING SHAMELESSLY, GRABBING ANYTHING THAT IS NOT NAILED DOWN.

THEY'RE PUFFS OF SMOKE PUSHED BY GUSTS OF WIND; LATE AUTUMN TREES STRIPPED CLEAN OF LEAF AND FRIUT, DOUBLY DEAD, PULLED UP BY THE ROOTS; WILD OCEAN WAVES LEAVING NOTHING ON THE BEACH, BUT THE FOAM OF SHAME; LOST STARS IN OUTER SPACE, ON THEIR WAY TO THE BLACK HOLE."

**Conclusion:**

Just as how pains tell us that something is wrong physically, and we seek medical assistance quickly, similarly, we must pay close attention to the painfulness that the BODY OF CHRIST is now experiencing. God has His specialists who can treat the severe VIRUSES OF OUR TIME. The world is scurrying to find a vaccine that will cure COVID-19, but we already have the vaccine that can cure THE SIN VIRUS. THE BLOOD OF JESUS CHRIST, and THE WORD OF GOD.

Remember we MUST treat the patients TENDERLY, but be TOUGH on sin virus.

Your Brother, Arthur Brown.


December 06, 2020

Precious Saints Greetings.

**Topic:** *WHAT BRINGS SWEETNESS TO A PASTOR.*

**Text:** 3 John 4 :

"I HAVE NO GREATER JOY THAN TO HEAR THAT MY CHILDREN WALK IN TRUTH."

**Introduction:**

A pastor's highest joy must come from knowing that his members are progressive in their Christian life. Many pastors are happy for what they can get materially out of the ministry. The Bible explicitly states that nobody should enter the ministry if he is GREEDY FOR FILTHY LUCRE. **1ˢᵗ Timothy 3:3,** and **1ˢᵗ Peter 5: 2.**

In our meditation today, I wish to point out four truths from our text.

A.  THE CONVERSION OF SOULS BRINGS SWEETNESS TO THE PASTOR.

A pastor can only call people: "MY CHILDREN" when he is the legitimate father. Too many pastors are none productive. We must remember that: CHILDREN ARE THE HERITAGE OF THE LORD, HAPPY IS THE MAN THAT HATH HIS QUIVER FULL OF THEM. **Psalm 127:3-5.** Every pastor should cry like Rachel in **Gen 30:1,** GIVE ME CHILDREN OR ELSE I DIE."

Every pastor MUST do the work of an evangelist. **2ⁿᵈ Timothy 4: 5.** Pastors are called TO BECOME FISHER'S OF MEN, NOT WATCHERS OF AQUARIUM.

B.  THE EDUCATION OF BELIEVERS IN TRUTH BRINGS SWEETNESS TO THE PASTOR.

The members MUST be taught the TRUTH before they can practice the TRUTH. It must be the holy ambition of every pastor that all of his members have a clear understanding of the ESSENTIAL, FUNDAMENTAL AND CARDINAL TRUTHS OF THE CHRISTIAN FAITH. The believers MUST be systematically taught the authenticity and inspiration of the HOLY SCRIPTURES. They will make the believers PROFITABLE in a toxic and polluted environment.

Paul clearly states in **1ˢᵗ Timothy 3:2** THE ABILITY TO TEACH IS ONE OF THE HIGHEST QUALIFICATIONS OF THE PASTOR. The early church grew rapidly because the leaders spent quality time in the MINISTRY OF THE WORD. **Acts 6: 4-7.** Every pastor must ensure that his members are well rooted and grounded in the TRUTH OF THE SCRIPTURES.

C. THE EXEMPLIFICATION OF TRUTH IN THE LIVES OF BELIEVERS BRINGS SWEETNESS TO THE PASTOR.

Every father is happy when a child resembles him or displays some of his characteristics. This dispels the fear of owning an illegitimate child. (OWNING A JACKET). Walking in TRUTH speaks of practical demonstrations of Christian living. The believers' adornment of the TRUTH must be visible. People saw it and were talking about what they saw. The report gladdened John's heart. We must remember that they also talk when believers stray and deviate from the TRUTH. The public life of the believer is very important. News was not spreading about their prayer life. Walking in TRUTH reveals the authenticity and genuineness of the believers. The church has been invaded by many counterfeit actors who are bringing PAINFULNESS INSTEAD OF SWEETNESS TO THEIR PASTORS.

The holiness of the Saints is the greatest means of spreading the gospel. **Acts 4: 13** says: "THEY TOOK KNOWLEDGE THAT THE DISCIPLES HAD BEEN WITH JESUS." These disciples TURNED THE WORLD UPSIDE DOWN **Acts 17: 6.**

ARE WALKING IN TRUTH.

The measure of our success is measured by the quality of our SUCCESSOR. Abraham had Isaac as his successor, David had Solomon as his successor and Paul had Timothy as his successor. Every genuine pastor wants to know that the work is in the hands of capable men when he is taken away. Moses knew that Joshua would have succeeded him, but it's extremely pathetic that we never heard of Joshua's successor. We should not be surprised then how shortly after he died; the nation went into APOSTASY AND ANARCHY. The highest reward any pastor can receive is TO HEAR THAT HIS MEMBERS ARE WALKING IN TRUTH. His precious children are making excellent spiritual progress. When that pastor stands before the throne of God, he will proudly present all his members to the Lord. **Hebrews 13:17.**

**Conclusion:**

Many pastors have suffered from days of anxiety and nights of sleeplessness because their members have denounced the TRUTH. Many were experiencing David's painfulness when he cried: "O ABSALOM, MY SON, MY SON, WOULD TO GOD I DIED FOR YOU." **2nd. Sam 18:33.** Moses loved his members so much that he said to God: "IF THOU WILT NOT FORGIVE THEIR SINS, BLOT ME, I PRAY THEE, OUT THY BOOK WHICH THOU HAS WRITTEN." **Exodus 32:32.**

Our members are superlatively blessed when they are walking zealously after good work, which is the authentication of genuine faith in Jesus Christ. This brings STUPENDOUS SWEETNESS TO THE PASTOR. HALLELUJAH.

Your Brother, Arthur Brown.

Sunday, December 13, 2020

Precious Saints Greetings.

**Topic:** Compassion is still apart of Christian's vocabulary

**Text:** James 1:27

"PURE RELIGION AND UNDEFILED BEFORE GOD AND THE FATHER IS THIS:"

"To visit the fatherless and widows in their affliction."

**Introduction:**

Christmas can be the loneliest time for many people. An increasing number of people seem to intensify some people's loneliness. Because of our human nature, we all need intimate relationships. When this need is not met, we become depressed. In our deprivation, we feel rejected and neglected. Many people are crying out like **Job** in **ch 31:35**, "OH THAT ONE WOULD HEAR ME." Job experienced the SILENCE AND HIDDENNESS OF GOD, which was extremely painful.

Our text clearly states that genuine Christianity is distinguished by THE CARE ITS ADHERENTS TAKE OF THE LESS FORTUNATE.

**Two activities are expected:**

1.  VISITATION OF THOSE SUFFERING AFFLICTION
2.  ALLEVIATION OF THEIR PAIN AND AFFLICTION.

JESUS' strong words in **Matthew 25:42-45** are still for Christians today:

"I WAS HUNGRY, AND HE GAVE ME NO MEAT: I WAS THIRSTY, AND YE GAVE ME NO DRINK: I WAS A STRANGER, AND YE TOOK ME NOT IN: NAKED, AND YE CLOTHED ME NOT: SICK, AND IN PRISON, AND YE VISITED ME NOT.

THEN SHALL THEY ANSWER HIM, SAYING, LORD, WHEN SAW WE THEE HUNGRY, OR THIRSTY, OR A STRANGER, OR NAKED, OR SICK, OR IN PRISON, AND DID NOT MINISTER UNTO THEE?

THEN SHALL HE ANSWER THEM, SAYING, VERILY I SAY UNTO YOU, INASMUCH AS YOU DID IT NOT TO ONE OF THE LEAST OF THESE, YE DID IT NOT TO ME."

The writer of Hebrews also says in **Ch 13: 2-3**

"BE NOT FORGETFUL TO ENTERTAIN STRANGERS: FOR THEREBY SOME HAVE ENTERTAINED ANGELS UNAWARES. REMEMBER THEM THAT ARE IN BONDS, AS BOUND WITH THEM; AND THEM WHICH SUFFER ADVERSITY, AS BEING YOURSELVES ALSO IN THE BODY."

**Conclusion:**

Jesus expects His followers to put on APRONS and serve suffering people. It is a fact that URBANIZATION HAS DESTROYED THE SPIRIT OF THE CARING COMMUNITY. Individuals feel lost in the crowd, especially now that all are wearing MASKS and can't even recognize one another.

Think carefully about these words of Henri J M Nouwen:

"WHAT WE SEE AND LIKE TO SEE IS CURE AND CHANGE. BUT WHAT WE DO NOT SEE AND DO NOT WANT TO SEE IS CARE, THE PARTICIPATION IN THE PAIN, THE SOLIDARITY IN THE SUFFERING, THE SHARING IN THE EXPERIENCE OF BROKENNESS. AND STILL, CURE WITHOUT CARE IS DEHUMANIZING A GIFT GIVEN WITH A COLD HEART."

This Christmas, don't give GIFTS WITH A COLD HEART. Instead, let's administer curative medication with a caring hand and a compassionate heart.

Let's all remember that the word COMPASSION is still in the vocabulary of Christianity.

Your Brother, Arthur Brown.

Sunday, December 29, 2020

Precious Saints Greetings.

**Topic:** Seven Great Titles Of Jesus in St John Ch one.

**Introduction:**

Solomon asked a very profound question: "BUT WILL GOD INDEED DWELL ON THE EARTH?" **1ˢᵗ Kings 8:27.** John the Apostle writes his gospel to give a resounding YES to Solomon's question. In chapter 1:14, John says: THE WORD WAS MADE FLESH, AND DWELT AMONG US, AND WE BEHELD HIS GLORY, THE GLORY OF THE ONLY BEGOTTEN OF THE FATHER, FULL OF GRACE AND TRUTH.

The four Gospel writers present Jesus in different ways.

(a) Matthew presents Him as KING OF THE JEWS.
(b) Mark presents Him as the BUSY SERVANT.
(c) Luke presents Him as the SYMPATHETIC SON OF GOD.
(d) John, the most theological of the writers, presents Jesus as THE SON OF GOD.

In chapter one of St John, we find SEVEN GREAT TITLES OF JESUS.

1. JESUS IS THE ESSENTIAL WORD ch 1: 1-3 and verse 14.

   (a) Jesus is the Eternal Word
   (b) Jesus is the creative Word
   (c) Jesus is the incarnate Word

2. JESUS IS THE BRIGHT LIGHT ch 1:4-13.

   He is the TRUE LIGHT. Satan is total darkness.

3. JESUS IS THE ONLY BEGOTTEN SON OF GOD ch 1:15-28, verse 49.

Many people in John's Gospel acknowledge the Deity of Jesus.

(a) John The Baptist in ch 1:34 says: "AND I SAW AND BARE RECORD THAT THIS IS THE SON OF GOD."
(b) Nathaniel said: "THOU ART THE SON OF GOD. ch 1: 49.
(c) Peter called Jesus, "CHRIST THE SON THE LIVING GOD." ch 6:69.
(d) The Blindman in Ch 9: 35-38 called Jesus "LORD" and worshipped Him.
(e) Martha called Him, "CHRIST THE SON OF GOD WHO SHOULD COME INTO THE WORLD."
(f) Thomas referred to Jesus as "MY LORD AND MY GOD." ch 20:28
(g) Jesus referred to Himself as "THE SON OF GOD" ch 5:25 and ch 10:36.

4. JESUS IS THE SACRIFICIAL LAMB OF GOD. Ch 1:29-34.

John The Baptist called Jesus, "THE LAMB OF GOD THAT TAKES AWAY THE SIN OF THE WORLD."

His baptism signifies the Death, Burial, and Resurrection of THE LAMB. Many years ago, Isaac asked: "WHERE IS THE LAMB?" Gen 22:7

In Rev 6: 16, the God rejectors will say: "HIDE US FROM THE WRATH OF THE LAMB.

5. JESUS IS THE PROMISED MESSIAH. Ch 1: 35-42.

John and Andrew ran to their brothers and excitingly announced: "WE HAVE FOUND THE MESSIAH WHICH IS INTERPRETED CHRIST OR THE ANOINTED ONE" v 41. Throughout the Old Testament, the Jews expected MESSIAH TO COME.

6. JESUS IS CROWNED KING OF ISRAEL. Ch 1:43-49.

Nathaniel, who was also called Bartholomew, called Jesus, "KING OF ISRAEL." V 49.

7. JESUS IS THE EXALTED SON OF MAN. V 51.

The Jews knew that this would be the special name for the promised Messiah ch 12:34.

Jesus is the LADDER between Heaven and earth. He is the God-Man bridging the gap between God and man.

**Conclusion:**

Instead of relating the birth narrative of Jesus, John takes us into ETERNITY PAST and reveals to us that Jesus existed with His Father before the world was formed. In his introductory chapter, John uses SEVEN TITLES, revealing that He was not an ordinary man, BUT GOD ROBED IN FLESH.

HE IS THE ESSENTIAL WORD
HE IS THE BRIGHT LIGHT
HE IS THE ONLY BEGOTTEN SON OF GOD
HE IS THE SACRIFICIAL LAMB OF GOD
HE IS THE PROMISED MESSIAH
HE IS THE CROWNED KING OF THE ISRAEL
HE IS THE EXALTED SON OF MAN.

John says anybody who accepts these TRUTHS has ETERNAL LIFE. Let's, therefore, fall before HIM like the shepherds and the wise men and WORSHIP JESUS AS OUR SAVIOUR AND LORD.

Your Brother, Arthur Brown.

Sunday, March 07, 2021

Precious Saints Greetings.

**Topic:** BIBLE READING IS THE ROAD TO REVIVAL.

**Text:** Deut 5:1

"AND MOSES CALLED ALL ISRAEL, AND SAID UNTO THEM, HEAR, O ISRAEL, THE STATUES AND JUDGMENTS WHICH I SPEAK IN YOUR EARS THIS DAY, THAT YE MAY LEARN THEM, AND KEEP THEM, AND DO THEM."

**Introduction:**

Satan's most effective weapon is allowing the church to drift along with the world. Like the time prior to Josiah's, the BIBLE is lost right in our churches. Entertainment has replaced religious education and spiritual edification. The nightclub-style has invaded the church. Dim lights and movie settings are now the order of the day. We must not aim at a peaceful coexistence with the devil's crowd. Instead, we must have a head-on collision. Many churches are encouraging people to leave their Bibles at home, for the scriptures will be projected on the screen. Let's be careful, less we programme people to neglect THEIR OWN BIBLES. Moses tells us in our text to do FOUR THINGS with the WORD OF GOD.

1. WE MUST HEAR THE WORD OF GOD. (get it in our ears).

Jesus in the parable of THE SOWER AND THE SEEDS teaches that 'THE EAR IS THE WAY TO A MAN' S HEART, St Matthew 13. In Matthew 7:22-24, Jesus says THE WISE MAN HEARS AND DOES THE WORD, BUT THE FOOLISH MAN HEARS BUT REJECTS THE WORD.

James tells us that we must hear the word of God (James 1:22-24.) Paul in Romans 10:17 says FAITH COMES BY THE HEARING OF THE WORD OF GOD.

Churches must therefore ensure that the word of God is read clearly to the people. Jesus spoke out the word of God for Satan to hear. Please remember that the word of God is the SWORD OF THE SPIRIT THAT WILL DEFEAT THE ENEMY. Ephesians 6:17.

In Nehemiah 8:8, the word of God was read DISTINCTLY to the people only if we could get back to a proliferation of the word of God in our homes, churches, and schools.

2. WE MUST LEARN THE WORD OF GOD. (get it in our head)

We must remember that REPETITION is one of the most effective methods of learning. There must be a great REVIVAL OF SCRIPTURE MEMORIZATION among believers today. Moses tells us how it should be done in Deut 6:6-9

"These words, which I command thee this day, shall be in thine heart: and thou shalt TEACH them DILIGENTLY unto thy children, and shalt TALK about them when thou sittest in thine house, and when thou walkest by the way, and when thou liest down, and when thou risest up.

Thou shalt BIND them for a sign upon thine hand, and they shall be as frontlets between thine eyes.

And thou shalt WRITE them upon the posts of thy house, and on thy gates."

Let's do it the way we learned OUR TIMETABLES.

3.  WE MUST KEEP THE WORD OF GOD. (get it in our heart).

    Psalm 119:11 tells us: "Thy word have I hid in mine HEART, that I might not sin against Thee.

    Remember to hide the BEST THING IN THE BEST PLACE FOR THE BEST PURPOSE.

    Hebrews 2:1 says, "We ought to give the MORE earnest heed to the things which we have heard, lest at any time we should let them slip."

    Pro 4:13 says: "Take fast hold of instruction, LET HER NOT GO: keep her, FOR SHE IS THY LIFE."

4.  WE MUST DO OR PRACTICE THE WORD OF GOD (get it in our hands and feet)

    James emphatically states that we should not just hear the word, but MUST DO THE WORD. James 1:22. In St John 15:14, Jesus says we are His FRIENDS IF WE DO whatsoever He commands us. Now we understand why Abraham was called THE FRIEND OF GOD several times in the Bible. He did anything God told him to Do. This was epitomized by his willingness to offer up his precious son Isaac, Gen 22.

    Many of us are CHALLENGED by the word of God but are not CHANGED by it. We are CONVICTED by it but are not CONVERTED by it. We must become PRACTICERS of the word.

**Conclusion:**

Two brothers were living in the same house, and both were DOCTORS. One was a medical doctor, and the other doctor of theology. One night an urgent call came requesting that DR BROWN should come quickly. "Which one do you want?" Asked the responder. "THE ONE THAT PRACTICES," came the reply.

Are we PRACTICERS OF THE WORD OF GOD or just faithful students of the word?

Moses gives us the simple sequence to follow:

1. HEAR THE WORD
2. LEARN THE WORD
3. KEEP THE WORD
4. DO THE WORD.

Your Brother, Arthur Brown.


Sunday, June 13, 2021

PRECIOUS SAINTS GREETINGS.

TOPIC: **THE UNIQUENESS AND MYSTERIOUSNESS OF THE MARITAL RELATIONSHIP.**

TEXT: **EPHESIANS 5:31-32.**

"FOR THIS CAUSE SHALL A MAN LEAVE HIS FATHER AND MOTHER, AND SHALL BE JOINED UNTO HIS WIFE, AND THEY TWO SHALL BE ONE FLESH.

THIS IS A GREAT MYSTERY: BUT I SPEAK CONCERNING CHRIST AND THE CHURCH."

**INTRODUCTION:**

Paul uses the metaphor of marriage to describe the relationship between Jesus and the church. Just as how Jesus loves the church: sacrificially, tenderly, and wholeheartedly, similarly, the husband must love his wife. The wife should be responsive to his love and reciprocate her love for him respectfully and unreservedly.

Today, we want to look at the MATHEMATICS OF MARRIAGE.

ONE + ONE = ONE

This speaks of the ONENESS IN MARRIAGE. But first, let's examine the FIVE AREAS OF ONENESS.

1.  ONENESS IN LOVE.

    Song Of Solomon 8: 6-7 says:

    "LOVE IS STRONG AS DEATH, THE COALS THEREOF ARE COALS OF FIRE, WHICH HATH A MOST VEHEMENT FLAME. MANY WATERS CANNOT QUENCH LOVE, NEITHER CAN FLOODS DROWN IT: IF A MAN WOULD GIVE ALL HIS SUBSTANCE OF HIS HOUSE FOR LOVE, IT WOULD UTTERLY BE CONTEMNED."

    Jesus loves His bride UNCONDITIONALLY, SACRIFICIALLY, AND ETERNALLY. The foundation of Marriage must be established on GENUINE LOVE, WHICH CANNOT BE QUENCHED OR DESTROYED. Love is the GREATEST OF ALL GRACES.

The fire of love must be constantly fueled with ATTENTION AND AFFECTION. It is the responsibility of the husband and his wife to add fuel OF LOVE TO THE FIRE OF MARRIAGE. Each one must add A BUNDLE OF LOVE STICK TO THE FIRE DAILY.

Beware of LUKEWARMNESS IN THE MARRIAGE. You are both PARTNERS AND LOVERS.

2.  ONENESS IN NAME.

According to James 2:7, "WE SHOULD NOT BLASPHEMY THAT WORTHY NAME BY WHICH WE ARE CALLED"

At a wedding ceremony, the minister makes a special announcement: "I NOW PRESENT TO YOU MR AND MRS (the husband's surname). There follow thunderous applause as they now have THE SAME NAME.

She is not ashamed of her NEW NAME. Instead, she writes it thereafter, UNASHAMEDLY.

Your name is important; it determines your identity.

Proverbs 22:1 says:

"A GOOD NAME IS RATHER TO BE CHOSEN THAN GREAT RICHES."

In Hebrews 11:24, the writer says: "WHEN MOSES WAS COME OF YEARS, HE REFUSED TO BE CALLED THE SON OF PHARAOH'S." Moses despised his EGYPTIAN NAME.

A husband must remember that HIS REPUTATION WILL AFFECT HIS SPOUSE'S REPUTATION because you both have the SAME NAME.

3.  ONENESS IN BODY.

According to Genesis 2: 21-25

EVE CAME FROM ADAM'S BODY. GOD JOINED THEM TOGETHER AS ONE FLESH IN MARRIAGE. THEY WERE NOT ASHAMED OF EACH OTHER'S BODY.

There must be a sacredness and expressiveness in marriage. Hebrews 13: 4 tells us: "MARRIAGE IS HONOURABLE IN ALL, THE BED IS UNDEFILED."

Solomon gives wise marital counseling in Proverbs 5: 15-21.

"Drink waters out thine own cistern, and running waters out of thine own well.
Let thy fountains be dispersed aboard, and rivers of waters in the streets.
Let them be only thine own, and not strangers' with thee.
Let thy fountain be blessed: and rejoice WITH THE WIFE OF THY YOUTH.
Let her be as the loving hind and pleasant roe,
Let her breasts satisfy thee at all times;
And be ravished always with her love.
And why wilt thou, my son, be ravished with a strange woman,
And embrace the bosom of a stranger?
FOR THE WAYS OF MAN ARE BEFORE THE EYES OF THE LORD,
AND HE PONDERETH ALL HIS GOINGS."

Also, in Song of Solomon 4:12-15 (TLB), he continues:

My darling is like a private garden,
A spring that no one can have,
A fountain of my own.
You are like a lovely orchard bearing precious fruit,
With the rarest of perfumes;
And saffron, calamus, and cinnamon,
And perfume from every other incense tree,
As well as myrrh and aloes, and every other lovely spice.
You are a garden fountain, a well of living water,
Refreshing as the streams from Lebanon mountains.

God expects FAITHFULNESS AND EXCLUSIVITY IN THE MARITAL RELATIONSHIP. In marriage, according to Paul, in 1 Corinthians 7:3-5

There is mutual OWNERSHIP of the body of each partner. Satan hates this UNIQUE ONENESS, and will make every effort to interrupt THE HARMONY OF YOUR SYMPHONY.

Each musician must play his/her instrument skillfully to bring pleasure to BODY, SOUL AND SPIRIT.

4.  ONENESS IN HOME.

Genesis 2: 24 "THEREFORE SHALL A MAN LEAVE HIS FATHER AND MOTHER, AND SHALL CLEAVE UNTO HIS WIFE."

Adam was not given a WIFE UNTIL HE HAD A SPECIAL GARDEN PREPARED FOR HER.

Many men are not ready for marriage because they are neither AMBITIOUS NOR INDUSTRIOUS. A real man wants to establish his own home and be the breadwinner and protector. The drum major instinct must be evident in a husband.

Just as how Jesus is the HEAD OF THE CHURCH, and provides QUALITY LEADERSHIP FOR HIS BRIDE, so a husband should provide quality LEADERSHIP FOR HIS HOME.

Christ is gone to PREPARE A HOME FOR HIS BRIDE. The marriage will take place when all THE PREPARATIONS ARE COMPLETED.

A home is a place of safety and security. Which good parents are willing to release their precious and beautiful daughter from THE NEST without knowing where she is being taken?

Let the Lord help you build that home. Psalm 127:1

5.  ONENESS IS POSSESSION.

According to Paul, in Ephesians 1:11, "THOSE WHO ARE IN CHRIST OBTAINED AN INHERITANCE." In Romans 8:16-17, THE BRIDE BECOMES HEIRS AND JOINT- HEIRS WITH CHRIST. The BRIDE is blessed with ALL SPIRITUAL BLESSINGS. Ephesians 1:3

When Abraham sent his servant to find a wife for his son Isaac, he sent:

TEN CAMELS LOADED WITH GOODS TO SHOW THE BRIDE A GLIMPSE OF THE WEALTH OF ISAAC. Genesis 24:10.

Ruth, the poverty-stricken widow, became instantly wealthy when she married Boaz.

At the wedding, the man repeats these words: "WITH THIS RING I THEE ENDOWED."

He is literally saying, "EVERYTHING THAT I OWN IS YOURS." The bride must also remember that when she puts a ring on the groom's finger, that is what she is saying.

FRIENDSHIP AND PARTNERSHIP MUST GOVERN YOUR MARRIAGE RELATIONSHIP.

## CONCLUSION:

Ecclesiastes 4:11 says: "IF TWO LIE TOGETHER, THEN THEY HAVE HEAT: BUT HOW CAN ONE BE WARM ALONE?"

There must be LOVE HEAT in your marriage. Beware of ALONENESS IN YOUR MARRIAGE that will lead to coldness and frigidity.

You may be celebrating another wedding anniversary; I implore you both, LIGHT YOUR CANDLE, SING A LOVE SONG TO EACH OTHER, AND FIND YOUR WAY BACK HOME TO YOUR FIRST LOVE.

Your Brother, Arthur Brown.

# SUMMARY

Once again, brethren, we bring greetings to you from God the Father of our Lord and His dear Son Jesus Christ. We believe that too many people's problems have affected their relationships and destroy marriages throughout the world. It is because we fail to follow God's directive for our lives, so we take on this project in writing to you and sharing God's word with you.

There are too many divorces in the Christain families, and some of our behavior is outrageous as if something is wrong with our mental ability to know right from wrong, knowing who we are in Christ Jesus and that we are bought with a great price. Jesus command peace in His children's live, brethren let us all pursue peace in our marriage.

In this book, we share with you what the word of God is saying to us that divorce is not the right thing to do and if you should divorce, you may not remarry according to the scripture; however, if you choose to remarry, go to your Lord your God and commune with Him. Therefore, come away from your ignorance and accept the word of God and husband love your wife unconditionally, and so is it with the wife; she must submit herself unto her husband as the head.

To the readers, please get you a Bible and follow along to verify the doctrine of this book that it is not the writer's doctrine, but instead, they are all God's word for your life and family. Unto the unsaved that may not know the scripture as should, as you read this book, please get a Bible and follow it to be at peace with the words you may not readily accept.

You may ask the question, what if I am in an abusive relationship? What should I do? These are crucial questions and need answers. Based upon the word of God, we cannot give you the advice to go against the word of God, but this we will say, and please pay attention. God shows you the person you are involved with, but you refuse the signs because you said it's love or sympathy.

You see how he treats you in private and public places, and you still stay. He beats you before marriage, and you still marry him.

You know how mean they were, but you still went on with the relationship. You know how disrespectful this man was to you, yet you still went on with the relationship and marriage.

You said he is a beast, but you still marry the beast; what? Did you think he was going to change, or maybe you can change him?

So, the best advice for Christian ladies is to marry a Christian man who loves the Lord, and the same goes for the men; knowing what the scripture said, we should not be an unequal yoke. But most of all, pray, and when you pray for each other, pray again.

You know that drinking was their problem, yet you went ahead with the relationship, not knowing it would worsen the marriage and cause terrible damage to family and others.

You know that drugs were the problem, yet you still went ahead with the relationship, and now there is hellfire in the relationship or marriage.

To the unsaved, marry someone that loves their parents and neighbors and pray. It is not easy to know who a person is because many are actors globally; they pretend to be the most excellent, sweet, and kind person until after the marriage, then you see Satan manifests himself in them, pray.

Whether you are a Christian or not, we all need God in our lives, and only Him can change people's hearts so that they can be loving to you and others; therefore, surrender your life and will unto Jesus, and He will give you a good life. But please, know this, as long as we are in this world full of sins, there will always be problems from Satan coming our way, but Jesus Christ will protect us from his onslaught. So don't worry; keep on praying to the God who is in heaven, and you will see the changes He is doing in your life and relationship. Then, when your breakthrough comes, don't stop praying because we are still flesh and bones, and it will always disappoint us. Since the Lord God does not want us to divorce our spouse, go to Him and tell Him what you are going through and that you are in need of His help, and He will come through for you; however, make sure that you are not at fault, if so, you need Jesus Christ first. While you are waiting on the Lord to work, have patience, read His Word, and pray. This is our advice to you and your family that is going through domestic horror but don't wait for a problem; take preventive measures by praying. Jesus Christ is our answer, and again, Jesus Christ is our only hope in this world.

One more crucial area needs to be addressed to all the female who is going through the life of what many call "hell on earth." This is the dwelling place that God the LORD gave to all of us as human beings to occupy until He comes back and fixes things back to their original state as they were from beginning.

There are many wives and single ladies whose life can be taken away from them at any time by their spouse, the man that they marry. Or those that are in a relationship waiting to be married at a later date. Domestic abuse in some homes is so poisonous that many children lose their precious, tender lives without knowing what has happened. Mothers kill their children out of frustrations, not able to cope with life because time is hard, and some don't see another way of escape from the pain, hurts, and suffering that they are getting from their husband or boyfriend.

Many lives have been wasted too early just because jealousy mixed with anger brings people into a state of rage, and hurting others seems at that time is the best thing to do. However, it is not so; please come to know the peacemaker. His name is Jesus Christ; He will help you by taking away the anger from the heart and give you peace like you never knew before.

If the wife leaves the husband, she can be in worse danger for her life because he will be in such a rage to kill, and if she stays sometimes, it is just a matter of time she will be no more. So what must they do, stay they die; if she leaves, they die—what a sad state for any person to be in, especially if there are children involved.

Please, men, it is not worth it to destroy life, and then yours will also be destroyed at the same time. So do not allow Satan, the devil, to use you as an instrument of destruction to hurt other human beings. Each year so many hospitalizations from domestic abuse at the hands of those that say that they love. Each year so many funeral services because she could not escape from death. Each year children have only one parent because of domestic abuse, and some have none.

If drinking is your problem, get professional help, there are many in the country you live in, we pray so. If drugs are the problem, get help, there is help out there; let somebody help you connect to them. If anger is your problem, get help; so many places and institutions can help you. But most important, get in touch with the Great Physician; His name is Jesus Christ. Tell Him all about your troubles. Let Him know that you cannot bear all of your problems by yourself. Tell Him that your burdens are too heavy for you to carry. Be honest to your God in heaven, sincerely call out to Him, and He will hear you. Please, let us save some lives in the precious name of Jesus because all lives are precious to Him.

Many thanks,

To God Be The Glory, AMEN.

www.ingramcontent.com/pod-product-compliance
Lightning Source LLC
Chambersburg PA
CBHW032233050726
47591CB00001B/383